C-1292   CAREER EXAMINATION SERIES

This is your
PASSBOOK for...

Garageman

Test Preparation Study Guide
Questions & Answers

COPYRIGHT NOTICE

This book is SOLELY intended for, is sold ONLY to, and its use is RESTRICTED to individual, bona fide applicants or candidates who qualify by virtue of having seriously filed applications for appropriate license, certificate, professional and/or promotional advancement, higher school matriculation, scholarship, or other legitimate requirements of education and/or governmental authorities.

This book is NOT intended for use, class instruction, tutoring, training, duplication, copying, reprinting, excerption, or adaptation, etc., by:

1) Other publishers
2) Proprietors and/or Instructors of "Coaching" and/or Preparatory Courses
3) Personnel and/or Training Divisions of commercial, industrial, and governmental organizations
4) Schools, colleges, or universities and/or their departments and staffs, including teachers and other personnel
5) Testing Agencies or Bureaus
6) Study groups which seek by the purchase of a single volume to copy and/or duplicate and/or adapt this material for use by the group as a whole without having purchased individual volumes for each of the members of the group
7) Et al.

Such persons would be in violation of appropriate Federal and State statutes.

PROVISION OF LICENSING AGREEMENTS – Recognized educational, commercial, industrial, and governmental institutions and organizations, and others legitimately engaged in educational pursuits, including training, testing, and measurement activities, may address request for a licensing agreement to the copyright owners, who will determine whether, and under what conditions, including fees and charges, the materials in this book may be used them. In other words, a licensing facility exists for the legitimate use of the material in this book on other than an individual basis. However, it is asseverated and affirmed here that the material in this book CANNOT be used without the receipt of the express permission of such a licensing agreement from the Publishers. Inquiries re licensing should be addressed to the company, attention rights and permissions department.

All rights reserved, including the right of reproduction in whole or in part, in any form or by any means, electronic or mechanical, including photocopying, recording, or by any information storage and retrieval system, without permission in writing from the Publisher.

Copyright © 2025 by
National Learning Corporation

212 Michael Drive, Syosset, NY 11791
(516) 921-8888 • www.passbooks.com
E-mail: info@passbooks.com

PASSBOOK® SERIES

THE *PASSBOOK® SERIES* has been created to prepare applicants and candidates for the ultimate academic battlefield – the examination room.

At some time in our lives, each and every one of us may be required to take an examination – for validation, matriculation, admission, qualification, registration, certification, or licensure.

Based on the assumption that every applicant or candidate has met the basic formal educational standards, has taken the required number of courses, and read the necessary texts, the *PASSBOOK® SERIES* furnishes the one special preparation which may assure passing with confidence, instead of failing with insecurity. Examination questions – together with answers – are furnished as the basic vehicle for study so that the mysteries of the examination and its compounding difficulties may be eliminated or diminished by a sure method.

This book is meant to help you pass your examination provided that you qualify and are serious in your objective.

The entire field is reviewed through the huge store of content information which is succinctly presented through a provocative and challenging approach – the question-and-answer method.

A climate of success is established by furnishing the correct answers at the end of each test.

You soon learn to recognize types of questions, forms of questions, and patterns of questioning. You may even begin to anticipate expected outcomes.

You perceive that many questions are repeated or adapted so that you can gain acute insights, which may enable you to score many sure points.

You learn how to confront new questions, or types of questions, and to attack them confidently and work out the correct answers.

You note objectives and emphases, and recognize pitfalls and dangers, so that you may make positive educational adjustments.

Moreover, you are kept fully informed in relation to new concepts, methods, practices, and directions in the field.

You discover that you are actually taking the examination all the time: you are preparing for the examination by "taking" an examination, not by reading extraneous and/or supererogatory textbooks.

In short, this PASSBOOK®, used directedly, should be an important factor in helping you to pass your test.

GARAGEMAN

JOB DUTIES:
　　A Garageman does general servicing and lubricating of cars, trucks and motorcycles; chauffeuring; parking cars; washing and waxing; may make minor repairs to vehicles; assists equipment mechanics by removing and replacing defective radiators, hoses, fan belts, and batteries; replaces tires on cars and trucks in the shop and in the field; may operate a light to heavy duty tow truck; and does other non-skilled tasks. Apprenticeships in various automotive crafts are available in some Garageman Attendant positions.

SCOPE OF EXAMINATION:
　　The examination will consist entirely of a written test comprised of multiple-choice questions, in which candidates may be examined for knowledge of: safe use of hand and air tools, such as pliers, wrenches, sockets sets, grease guns, impact wrench, air tire changer; safe operation of lifting equipment/devices, such as hoists, floor jacks, and safety stands; various types of lubricants, oils, and greases used in performing routine vehicle maintenance; routine shop or garage maintenance such as proper use and storage of cleaning solvents, general shop clean up; tire maintenance and repair procedures, including the safe and proper use of tire repair tools and supplies; routine battery maintenance; safe charging or jump starting procedures, such as locating positive/negative terminals; connecting cables to proper terminals; ability to: recognize major engine components and accessories on vehicles; check the fluid level of various operating systems, such as the cooling system, brakes, and power steering; perform routine vehicle maintenance; safely operate a variety of light vehicles; read maps and/or interpret written directional instructions; read and interpret information from written materials; maintain routine written records or reports on vehicle repairs and maintenance; follow basic instructions, verbally or in writing; and other necessary skills, knowledge, and abilities.

HOW TO TAKE A TEST

I. YOU MUST PASS AN EXAMINATION

A. WHAT EVERY CANDIDATE SHOULD KNOW

Examination applicants often ask us for help in preparing for the written test. What can I study in advance? What kinds of questions will be asked? How will the test be given? How will the papers be graded?

As an applicant for a civil service examination, you may be wondering about some of these things. Our purpose here is to suggest effective methods of advance study and to describe civil service examinations.

Your chances for success on this examination can be increased if you know how to prepare. Those "pre-examination jitters" can be reduced if you know what to expect. You can even experience an adventure in good citizenship if you know why civil service exams are given.

B. WHY ARE CIVIL SERVICE EXAMINATIONS GIVEN?

Civil service examinations are important to you in two ways. As a citizen, you want public jobs filled by employees who know how to do their work. As a job seeker, you want a fair chance to compete for that job on an equal footing with other candidates. The best-known means of accomplishing this two-fold goal is the competitive examination.

Exams are widely publicized throughout the nation. They may be administered for jobs in federal, state, city, municipal, town or village governments or agencies.

Any citizen may apply, with some limitations, such as the age or residence of applicants. Your experience and education may be reviewed to see whether you meet the requirements for the particular examination. When these requirements exist, they are reasonable and applied consistently to all applicants. Thus, a competitive examination may cause you some uneasiness now, but it is your privilege and safeguard.

C. HOW ARE CIVIL SERVICE EXAMS DEVELOPED?

Examinations are carefully written by trained technicians who are specialists in the field known as "psychological measurement," in consultation with recognized authorities in the field of work that the test will cover. These experts recommend the subject matter areas or skills to be tested; only those knowledges or skills important to your success on the job are included. The most reliable books and source materials available are used as references. Together, the experts and technicians judge the difficulty level of the questions.

Test technicians know how to phrase questions so that the problem is clearly stated. Their ethics do not permit "trick" or "catch" questions. Questions may have been tried out on sample groups, or subjected to statistical analysis, to determine their usefulness.

Written tests are often used in combination with performance tests, ratings of training and experience, and oral interviews. All of these measures combine to form the best-known means of finding the right person for the right job.

II. HOW TO PASS THE WRITTEN TEST

A. NATURE OF THE EXAMINATION

To prepare intelligently for civil service examinations, you should know how they differ from school examinations you have taken. In school you were assigned certain definite pages to read or subjects to cover. The examination questions were quite detailed and usually emphasized memory. Civil service exams, on the other hand, try to discover your present ability to perform the duties of a position, plus your potentiality to learn these duties. In other words, a civil service exam attempts to predict how successful you will be. Questions cover such a broad area that they cannot be as minute and detailed as school exam questions.

In the public service similar kinds of work, or positions, are grouped together in one "class." This process is known as *position-classification*. All the positions in a class are paid according to the salary range for that class. One class title covers all of these positions, and they are all tested by the same examination.

B. FOUR BASIC STEPS

1) Study the announcement

How, then, can you know what subjects to study? Our best answer is: "Learn as much as possible about the class of positions for which you've applied." The exam will test the knowledge, skills and abilities needed to do the work.

Your most valuable source of information about the position you want is the official exam announcement. This announcement lists the training and experience qualifications. Check these standards and apply only if you come reasonably close to meeting them.

The brief description of the position in the examination announcement offers some clues to the subjects which will be tested. Think about the job itself. Review the duties in your mind. Can you perform them, or are there some in which you are rusty? Fill in the blank spots in your preparation.

Many jurisdictions preview the written test in the exam announcement by including a section called "Knowledge and Abilities Required," "Scope of the Examination," or some similar heading. Here you will find out specifically what fields will be tested.

2) Review your own background

Once you learn in general what the position is all about, and what you need to know to do the work, ask yourself which subjects you already know fairly well and which need improvement. You may wonder whether to concentrate on improving your strong areas or on building some background in your fields of weakness. When the announcement has specified "some knowledge" or "considerable knowledge," or has used adjectives like "beginning principles of..." or "advanced ... methods," you can get a clue as to the number and difficulty of questions to be asked in any given field. More questions, and hence broader coverage, would be included for those subjects which are more important in the work. Now weigh your strengths and weaknesses against the job requirements and prepare accordingly.

3) Determine the level of the position

Another way to tell how intensively you should prepare is to understand the level of the job for which you are applying. Is it the entering level? In other words, is this the position in which beginners in a field of work are hired? Or is it an intermediate or advanced level? Sometimes this is indicated by such words as "Junior" or "Senior" in the class title. Other jurisdictions use Roman numerals to designate the level – Clerk I, Clerk II, for example. The word "Supervisor" sometimes appears in the title. If the level is not indicated by the title, check the description of duties. Will you be working under very close supervision, or will you have responsibility for independent decisions in this work?

4) Choose appropriate study materials

Now that you know the subjects to be examined and the relative amount of each subject to be covered, you can choose suitable study materials. For beginning level jobs, or even advanced ones, if you have a pronounced weakness in some aspect of your training, read a modern, standard textbook in that field. Be sure it is up to date and has general coverage. Such books are normally available at your library, and the librarian will be glad to help you locate one. For entry-level positions, questions of appropriate difficulty are chosen – neither highly advanced questions, nor those too simple. Such questions require careful thought but not advanced training.

If the position for which you are applying is technical or advanced, you will read more advanced, specialized material. If you are already familiar with the basic principles of your field, elementary textbooks would waste your time. Concentrate on advanced textbooks and technical periodicals. Think through the concepts and review difficult problems in your field.

These are all general sources. You can get more ideas on your own initiative, following these leads. For example, training manuals and publications of the government agency which employs workers in your field can be useful, particularly for technical and professional positions. A letter or visit to the government department involved may result in more specific study suggestions, and certainly will provide you with a more definite idea of the exact nature of the position you are seeking.

III. KINDS OF TESTS

Tests are used for purposes other than measuring knowledge and ability to perform specified duties. For some positions, it is equally important to test ability to make adjustments to new situations or to profit from training. In others, basic mental abilities not dependent on information are essential. Questions which test these things may not appear as pertinent to the duties of the position as those which test for knowledge and information. Yet they are often highly important parts of a fair examination. For very general questions, it is almost impossible to help you direct your study efforts. What we can do is to point out some of the more common of these general abilities needed in public service positions and describe some typical questions.

1) General information

Broad, general information has been found useful for predicting job success in some kinds of work. This is tested in a variety of ways, from vocabulary lists to questions about current events. Basic background in some field of work, such as sociology or economics, may be sampled in a group of questions. Often these are principles which have become familiar to most persons through exposure rather than through formal training. It is difficult to advise you how to study for these questions; being alert to the world around you is our best suggestion.

2) Verbal ability

An example of an ability needed in many positions is verbal or language ability. Verbal ability is, in brief, the ability to use and understand words. Vocabulary and grammar tests are typical measures of this ability. Reading comprehension or paragraph interpretation questions are common in many kinds of civil service tests. You are given a paragraph of written material and asked to find its central meaning.

3) Numerical ability

Number skills can be tested by the familiar arithmetic problem, by checking paired lists of numbers to see which are alike and which are different, or by interpreting charts and graphs. In the latter test, a graph may be printed in the test booklet which you are asked to use as the basis for answering questions.

4) Observation

A popular test for law-enforcement positions is the observation test. A picture is shown to you for several minutes, then taken away. Questions about the picture test your ability to observe both details and larger elements.

5) Following directions

In many positions in the public service, the employee must be able to carry out written instructions dependably and accurately. You may be given a chart with several columns, each column listing a variety of information. The questions require you to carry out directions involving the information given in the chart.

6) Skills and aptitudes

Performance tests effectively measure some manual skills and aptitudes. When the skill is one in which you are trained, such as typing or shorthand, you can practice. These tests are often very much like those given in business school or high school courses. For many of the other skills and aptitudes, however, no short-time preparation can be made. Skills and abilities natural to you or that you have developed throughout your lifetime are being tested.

Many of the general questions just described provide all the data needed to answer the questions and ask you to use your reasoning ability to find the answers. Your best preparation for these tests, as well as for tests of facts and ideas, is to be at your physical and mental best. You, no doubt, have your own methods of getting into an exam-taking mood and keeping "in shape." The next section lists some ideas on this subject.

IV. KINDS OF QUESTIONS

Only rarely is the "essay" question, which you answer in narrative form, used in civil service tests. Civil service tests are usually of the short-answer type. Full instructions for answering these questions will be given to you at the examination. But in case this is your first experience with short-answer questions and separate answer sheets, here is what you need to know:

1) Multiple-choice Questions

Most popular of the short-answer questions is the "multiple choice" or "best answer" question. It can be used, for example, to test for factual knowledge, ability to solve problems or judgment in meeting situations found at work.

A multiple-choice question is normally one of three types—

- It can begin with an incomplete statement followed by several possible endings. You are to find the one ending which *best* completes the statement, although some of the others may not be entirely wrong.
- It can also be a complete statement in the form of a question which is answered by choosing one of the statements listed.

- It can be in the form of a problem – again you select the best answer.

Here is an example of a multiple-choice question with a discussion which should give you some clues as to the method for choosing the right answer:

When an employee has a complaint about his assignment, the action which will *best* help him overcome his difficulty is to
   A. discuss his difficulty with his coworkers
   B. take the problem to the head of the organization
   C. take the problem to the person who gave him the assignment
   D. say nothing to anyone about his complaint

In answering this question, you should study each of the choices to find which is best. Consider choice "A" – Certainly an employee may discuss his complaint with fellow employees, but no change or improvement can result, and the complaint remains unresolved. Choice "B" is a poor choice since the head of the organization probably does not know what assignment you have been given, and taking your problem to him is known as "going over the head" of the supervisor. The supervisor, or person who made the assignment, is the person who can clarify it or correct any injustice. Choice "C" is, therefore, correct. To say nothing, as in choice "D," is unwise. Supervisors have and interest in knowing the problems employees are facing, and the employee is seeking a solution to his problem.

2) True/False Questions

The "true/false" or "right/wrong" form of question is sometimes used. Here a complete statement is given. Your job is to decide whether the statement is right or wrong.

SAMPLE: A roaming cell-phone call to a nearby city costs less than a non-roaming call to a distant city.

This statement is wrong, or false, since roaming calls are more expensive.

This is not a complete list of all possible question forms, although most of the others are variations of these common types. You will always get complete directions for answering questions. Be sure you understand *how* to mark your answers – ask questions until you do.

V. RECORDING YOUR ANSWERS

Computer terminals are used more and more today for many different kinds of exams.

For an examination with very few applicants, you may be told to record your answers in the test booklet itself. Separate answer sheets are much more common. If this separate answer sheet is to be scored by machine – and this is often the case – it is highly important that you mark your answers correctly in order to get credit.

An electronic scoring machine is often used in civil service offices because of the speed with which papers can be scored. Machine-scored answer sheets must be marked with a pencil, which will be given to you. This pencil has a high graphite content which responds to the electronic scoring machine. As a matter of fact, stray dots may register as answers, so do not let your pencil rest on the answer sheet while you are pondering the correct answer. Also, if your pencil lead breaks or is otherwise defective, ask for another.

Since the answer sheet will be dropped in a slot in the scoring machine, be careful not to bend the corners or get the paper crumpled.

The answer sheet normally has five vertical columns of numbers, with 30 numbers to a column. These numbers correspond to the question numbers in your test booklet. After each number, going across the page are four or five pairs of dotted lines. These short dotted lines have small letters or numbers above them. The first two pairs may also have a "T" or "F" above the letters. This indicates that the first two pairs only are to be used if the questions are of the true-false type. If the questions are multiple choice, disregard the "T" and "F" and pay attention only to the small letters or numbers.

Answer your questions in the manner of the sample that follows:

32. The largest city in the United States is
    A. Washington, D.C.
    B. New York City
    C. Chicago
    D. Detroit
    E. San Francisco

1) Choose the answer you think is best. (New York City is the largest, so "B" is correct.)
2) Find the row of dotted lines numbered the same as the question you are answering. (Find row number 32)
3) Find the pair of dotted lines corresponding to the answer. (Find the pair of lines under the mark "B.")
4) Make a solid black mark between the dotted lines.

VI. BEFORE THE TEST

Common sense will help you find procedures to follow to get ready for an examination. Too many of us, however, overlook these sensible measures. Indeed, nervousness and fatigue have been found to be the most serious reasons why applicants fail to do their best on civil service tests. Here is a list of reminders:

- Begin your preparation early – Don't wait until the last minute to go scurrying around for books and materials or to find out what the position is all about.
- Prepare continuously – An hour a night for a week is better than an all-night cram session. This has been definitely established. What is more, a night a week for a month will return better dividends than crowding your study into a shorter period of time.
- Locate the place of the exam – You have been sent a notice telling you when and where to report for the examination. If the location is in a different town or otherwise unfamiliar to you, it would be well to inquire the best route and learn something about the building.
- Relax the night before the test – Allow your mind to rest. Do not study at all that night. Plan some mild recreation or diversion; then go to bed early and get a good night's sleep.
- Get up early enough to make a leisurely trip to the place for the test – This way unforeseen events, traffic snarls, unfamiliar buildings, etc. will not upset you.
- Dress comfortably – A written test is not a fashion show. You will be known by number and not by name, so wear something comfortable.

- Leave excess paraphernalia at home – Shopping bags and odd bundles will get in your way. You need bring only the items mentioned in the official notice you received; usually everything you need is provided. Do not bring reference books to the exam. They will only confuse those last minutes and be taken away from you when in the test room.
- Arrive somewhat ahead of time – If because of transportation schedules you must get there very early, bring a newspaper or magazine to take your mind off yourself while waiting.
- Locate the examination room – When you have found the proper room, you will be directed to the seat or part of the room where you will sit. Sometimes you are given a sheet of instructions to read while you are waiting. Do not fill out any forms until you are told to do so; just read them and be prepared.
- Relax and prepare to listen to the instructions
- If you have any physical problem that may keep you from doing your best, be sure to tell the test administrator. If you are sick or in poor health, you really cannot do your best on the exam. You can come back and take the test some other time.

VII. AT THE TEST

The day of the test is here and you have the test booklet in your hand. The temptation to get going is very strong. Caution! There is more to success than knowing the right answers. You must know how to identify your papers and understand variations in the type of short-answer question used in this particular examination. Follow these suggestions for maximum results from your efforts:

1) Cooperate with the monitor

The test administrator has a duty to create a situation in which you can be as much at ease as possible. He will give instructions, tell you when to begin, check to see that you are marking your answer sheet correctly, and so on. He is not there to guard you, although he will see that your competitors do not take unfair advantage. He wants to help you do your best.

2) Listen to all instructions

Don't jump the gun! Wait until you understand all directions. In most civil service tests you get more time than you need to answer the questions. So don't be in a hurry. Read each word of instructions until you clearly understand the meaning. Study the examples, listen to all announcements and follow directions. Ask questions if you do not understand what to do.

3) Identify your papers

Civil service exams are usually identified by number only. You will be assigned a number; you must not put your name on your test papers. Be sure to copy your number correctly. Since more than one exam may be given, copy your exact examination title.

4) Plan your time

Unless you are told that a test is a "speed" or "rate of work" test, speed itself is usually not important. Time enough to answer all the questions will be provided, but this does not mean that you have all day. An overall time limit has been set. Divide the total time (in minutes) by the number of questions to determine the approximate time you have for each question.

5) Do not linger over difficult questions

If you come across a difficult question, mark it with a paper clip (useful to have along) and come back to it when you have been through the booklet. One caution if you do this – be sure to skip a number on your answer sheet as well. Check often to be sure that you have not lost your place and that you are marking in the row numbered the same as the question you are answering.

6) Read the questions

Be sure you know what the question asks! Many capable people are unsuccessful because they failed to *read* the questions correctly.

7) Answer all questions

Unless you have been instructed that a penalty will be deducted for incorrect answers, it is better to guess than to omit a question.

8) Speed tests

It is often better NOT to guess on speed tests. It has been found that on timed tests people are tempted to spend the last few seconds before time is called in marking answers at random – without even reading them – in the hope of picking up a few extra points. To discourage this practice, the instructions may warn you that your score will be "corrected" for guessing. That is, a penalty will be applied. The incorrect answers will be deducted from the correct ones, or some other penalty formula will be used.

9) Review your answers

If you finish before time is called, go back to the questions you guessed or omitted to give them further thought. Review other answers if you have time.

10) Return your test materials

If you are ready to leave before others have finished or time is called, take ALL your materials to the monitor and leave quietly. Never take any test material with you. The monitor can discover whose papers are not complete, and taking a test booklet may be grounds for disqualification.

VIII. EXAMINATION TECHNIQUES

1) Read the general instructions carefully. These are usually printed on the first page of the exam booklet. As a rule, these instructions refer to the timing of the examination; the fact that you should not start work until the signal and must stop work at a signal, etc. If there are any *special* instructions, such as a choice of questions to be answered, make sure that you note this instruction carefully.

2) When you are ready to start work on the examination, that is as soon as the signal has been given, read the instructions to each question booklet, underline any key words or phrases, such as *least, best, outline, describe* and the like. In this way you will tend to answer as requested rather than discover on reviewing your paper that you *listed without describing*, that you selected the *worst* choice rather than the *best* choice, etc.

3) If the examination is of the objective or multiple-choice type – that is, each question will also give a series of possible answers: A, B, C or D, and you are called upon to select the best answer and write the letter next to that answer on your answer paper – it is advisable to start answering each question in turn. There may be anywhere from 50 to 100 such questions in the three or four hours allotted and you can see how much time would be taken if you read through all the questions before beginning to answer any. Furthermore, if you come across a question or group of questions which you know would be difficult to answer, it would undoubtedly affect your handling of all the other questions.

4) If the examination is of the essay type and contains but a few questions, it is a moot point as to whether you should read all the questions before starting to answer any one. Of course, if you are given a choice – say five out of seven and the like – then it is essential to read all the questions so you can eliminate the two that are most difficult. If, however, you are asked to answer all the questions, there may be danger in trying to answer the easiest one first because you may find that you will spend too much time on it. The best technique is to answer the first question, then proceed to the second, etc.

5) Time your answers. Before the exam begins, write down the time it started, then add the time allowed for the examination and write down the time it must be completed, then divide the time available somewhat as follows:
    - If 3-1/2 hours are allowed, that would be 210 minutes. If you have 80 objective-type questions, that would be an average of 2-1/2 minutes per question. Allow yourself no more than 2 minutes per question, or a total of 160 minutes, which will permit about 50 minutes to review.
    - If for the time allotment of 210 minutes there are 7 essay questions to answer, that would average about 30 minutes a question. Give yourself only 25 minutes per question so that you have about 35 minutes to review.

6) The most important instruction is to *read each question* and make sure you know what is wanted. The second most important instruction is to *time yourself properly* so that you answer every question. The third most important instruction is to *answer every question*. Guess if you have to but include something for each question. Remember that you will receive no credit for a blank and will probably receive some credit if you write something in answer to an essay question. If you guess a letter – say "B" for a multiple-choice question – you may have guessed right. If you leave a blank as an answer to a multiple-choice question, the examiners may respect your feelings but it will not add a point to your score. Some exams may penalize you for wrong answers, so in such cases *only*, you may not want to guess unless you have some basis for your answer.

7) Suggestions
    a. Objective-type questions
        1. Examine the question booklet for proper sequence of pages and questions
        2. Read all instructions carefully
        3. Skip any question which seems too difficult; return to it after all other questions have been answered
        4. Apportion your time properly; do not spend too much time on any single question or group of questions

5. Note and underline key words – *all, most, fewest, least, best, worst, same, opposite*, etc.
6. Pay particular attention to negatives
7. Note unusual option, e.g., unduly long, short, complex, different or similar in content to the body of the question
8. Observe the use of "hedging" words – *probably, may, most likely*, etc.
9. Make sure that your answer is put next to the same number as the question
10. Do not second-guess unless you have good reason to believe the second answer is definitely more correct
11. Cross out original answer if you decide another answer is more accurate; do not erase until you are ready to hand your paper in
12. Answer all questions; guess unless instructed otherwise
13. Leave time for review

b. Essay questions
1. Read each question carefully
2. Determine exactly what is wanted. Underline key words or phrases.
3. Decide on outline or paragraph answer
4. Include many different points and elements unless asked to develop any one or two points or elements
5. Show impartiality by giving pros and cons unless directed to select one side only
6. Make and write down any assumptions you find necessary to answer the questions
7. Watch your English, grammar, punctuation and choice of words
8. Time your answers; don't crowd material

8) Answering the essay question

Most essay questions can be answered by framing the specific response around several key words or ideas. Here are a few such key words or ideas:

M's: manpower, materials, methods, money, management
P's: purpose, program, policy, plan, procedure, practice, problems, pitfalls, personnel, public relations

a. Six basic steps in handling problems:
1. Preliminary plan and background development
2. Collect information, data and facts
3. Analyze and interpret information, data and facts
4. Analyze and develop solutions as well as make recommendations
5. Prepare report and sell recommendations
6. Install recommendations and follow up effectiveness

b. Pitfalls to avoid
1. *Taking things for granted* – A statement of the situation does not necessarily imply that each of the elements is necessarily true; for example, a complaint may be invalid and biased so that all that can be taken for granted is that a complaint has been registered

2. *Considering only one side of a situation* – Wherever possible, indicate several alternatives and then point out the reasons you selected the best one
3. *Failing to indicate follow up* – Whenever your answer indicates action on your part, make certain that you will take proper follow-up action to see how successful your recommendations, procedures or actions turn out to be
4. *Taking too long in answering any single question* – Remember to time your answers properly

IX. AFTER THE TEST

Scoring procedures differ in detail among civil service jurisdictions although the general principles are the same. Whether the papers are hand-scored or graded by machine we have described, they are nearly always graded by number. That is, the person who marks the paper knows only the number – never the name – of the applicant. Not until all the papers have been graded will they be matched with names. If other tests, such as training and experience or oral interview ratings have been given, scores will be combined. Different parts of the examination usually have different weights. For example, the written test might count 60 percent of the final grade, and a rating of training and experience 40 percent. In many jurisdictions, veterans will have a certain number of points added to their grades.

After the final grade has been determined, the names are placed in grade order and an eligible list is established. There are various methods for resolving ties between those who get the same final grade – probably the most common is to place first the name of the person whose application was received first. Job offers are made from the eligible list in the order the names appear on it. You will be notified of your grade and your rank as soon as all these computations have been made. This will be done as rapidly as possible.

People who are found to meet the requirements in the announcement are called "eligibles." Their names are put on a list of eligible candidates. An eligible's chances of getting a job depend on how high he stands on this list and how fast agencies are filling jobs from the list.

When a job is to be filled from a list of eligibles, the agency asks for the names of people on the list of eligibles for that job. When the civil service commission receives this request, it sends to the agency the names of the three people highest on this list. Or, if the job to be filled has specialized requirements, the office sends the agency the names of the top three persons who meet these requirements from the general list.

The appointing officer makes a choice from among the three people whose names were sent to him. If the selected person accepts the appointment, the names of the others are put back on the list to be considered for future openings.

That is the rule in hiring from all kinds of eligible lists, whether they are for typist, carpenter, chemist, or something else. For every vacancy, the appointing officer has his choice of any one of the top three eligibles on the list. This explains why the person whose name is on top of the list sometimes does not get an appointment when some of the persons lower on the list do. If the appointing officer chooses the second or third eligible, the No. 1 eligible does not get a job at once, but stays on the list until he is appointed or the list is terminated.

X. HOW TO PASS THE INTERVIEW TEST

The examination for which you applied requires an oral interview test. You have already taken the written test and you are now being called for the interview test – the final part of the formal examination.

You may think that it is not possible to prepare for an interview test and that there are no procedures to follow during an interview. Our purpose is to point out some things you can do in advance that will help you and some good rules to follow and pitfalls to avoid while you are being interviewed.

What is an interview supposed to test?

The written examination is designed to test the technical knowledge and competence of the candidate; the oral is designed to evaluate intangible qualities, not readily measured otherwise, and to establish a list showing the relative fitness of each candidate – as measured against his competitors – for the position sought. Scoring is not on the basis of "right" and "wrong," but on a sliding scale of values ranging from "not passable" to "outstanding." As a matter of fact, it is possible to achieve a relatively low score without a single "incorrect" answer because of evident weakness in the qualities being measured.

Occasionally, an examination may consist entirely of an oral test – either an individual or a group oral. In such cases, information is sought concerning the technical knowledges and abilities of the candidate, since there has been no written examination for this purpose. More commonly, however, an oral test is used to supplement a written examination.

Who conducts interviews?

The composition of oral boards varies among different jurisdictions. In nearly all, a representative of the personnel department serves as chairman. One of the members of the board may be a representative of the department in which the candidate would work. In some cases, "outside experts" are used, and, frequently, a businessman or some other representative of the general public is asked to serve. Labor and management or other special groups may be represented. The aim is to secure the services of experts in the appropriate field.

However the board is composed, it is a good idea (and not at all improper or unethical) to ascertain in advance of the interview who the members are and what groups they represent. When you are introduced to them, you will have some idea of their backgrounds and interests, and at least you will not stutter and stammer over their names.

What should be done before the interview?

While knowledge about the board members is useful and takes some of the surprise element out of the interview, there is other preparation which is more substantive. It *is* possible to prepare for an oral interview – in several ways:

1) Keep a copy of your application and review it carefully before the interview

This may be the only document before the oral board, and the starting point of the interview. Know what education and experience you have listed there, and the sequence and dates of all of it. Sometimes the board will ask you to review the highlights of your experience for them; you should not have to hem and haw doing it.

2) Study the class specification and the examination announcement

Usually, the oral board has one or both of these to guide them. The qualities, characteristics or knowledges required by the position sought are stated in these documents. They offer valuable clues as to the nature of the oral interview. For example, if the job involves supervisory responsibilities, the announcement will usually indicate that knowledge of modern supervisory methods and the qualifications of the candidate as a supervisor will be tested. If so, you can expect such questions, frequently in the form of a hypothetical situation which you are expected to solve. NEVER go into an oral without knowledge of the duties and responsibilities of the job you seek.

3) Think through each qualification required

Try to visualize the kind of questions you would ask if you were a board member. How well could you answer them? Try especially to appraise your own knowledge and background in each area, *measured against the job sought*, and identify any areas in which you are weak. Be critical and realistic – do not flatter yourself.

4) Do some general reading in areas in which you feel you may be weak

For example, if the job involves supervision and your past experience has NOT, some general reading in supervisory methods and practices, particularly in the field of human relations, might be useful. Do NOT study agency procedures or detailed manuals. The oral board will be testing your understanding and capacity, not your memory.

5) Get a good night's sleep and watch your general health and mental attitude

You will want a clear head at the interview. Take care of a cold or any other minor ailment, and of course, no hangovers.

What should be done on the day of the interview?

Now comes the day of the interview itself. Give yourself plenty of time to get there. Plan to arrive somewhat ahead of the scheduled time, particularly if your appointment is in the fore part of the day. If a previous candidate fails to appear, the board might be ready for you a bit early. By early afternoon an oral board is almost invariably behind schedule if there are many candidates, and you may have to wait. Take along a book or magazine to read, or your application to review, but leave any extraneous material in the waiting room when you go in for your interview. In any event, relax and compose yourself.

The matter of dress is important. The board is forming impressions about you – from your experience, your manners, your attitude, and your appearance. Give your personal appearance careful attention. Dress your best, but not your flashiest. Choose conservative, appropriate clothing, and be sure it is immaculate. This is a business interview, and your appearance should indicate that you regard it as such. Besides, being well groomed and properly dressed will help boost your confidence.

Sooner or later, someone will call your name and escort you into the interview room. *This is it.* From here on you are on your own. It is too late for any more preparation. But remember, you asked for this opportunity to prove your fitness, and you are here because your request was granted.

What happens when you go in?

The usual sequence of events will be as follows: The clerk (who is often the board stenographer) will introduce you to the chairman of the oral board, who will introduce you to the other members of the board. Acknowledge the introductions before you sit down. Do not be surprised if you find a microphone facing you or a stenotypist sitting by. Oral interviews are usually recorded in the event of an appeal or other review.

Usually the chairman of the board will open the interview by reviewing the highlights of your education and work experience from your application – primarily for the benefit of the other members of the board, as well as to get the material into the record. Do not interrupt or comment unless there is an error or significant misinterpretation; if that is the case, do not hesitate. But do not quibble about insignificant matters. Also, he will usually ask you some question about your education, experience or your present job – partly to get you to start talking and to establish the interviewing "rapport." He may start the actual questioning, or turn it over to one of the other members. Frequently, each member undertakes the questioning on a particular area, one in which he is perhaps most competent, so you can expect each member to participate in the examination. Because time is limited, you may also expect some rather abrupt switches in the direction the questioning takes, so do not be upset by it. Normally, a board member will not pursue a single line of questioning unless he discovers a particular strength or weakness.

After each member has participated, the chairman will usually ask whether any member has any further questions, then will ask you if you have anything you wish to add. Unless you are expecting this question, it may floor you. Worse, it may start you off on an extended, extemporaneous speech. The board is not usually seeking more information. The question is principally to offer you a last opportunity to present further qualifications or to indicate that you have nothing to add. So, if you feel that a significant qualification or characteristic has been overlooked, it is proper to point it out in a sentence or so. Do not compliment the board on the thoroughness of their examination – they have been sketchy, and you know it. If you wish, merely say, "No thank you, I have nothing further to add." This is a point where you can "talk yourself out" of a good impression or fail to present an important bit of information. Remember, *you close the interview yourself.*

The chairman will then say, "That is all, Mr. _____, thank you." Do not be startled; the interview is over, and quicker than you think. Thank him, gather your belongings and take your leave. Save your sigh of relief for the other side of the door.

How to put your best foot forward

Throughout this entire process, you may feel that the board individually and collectively is trying to pierce your defenses, seek out your hidden weaknesses and embarrass and confuse you. Actually, this is not true. They are obliged to make an appraisal of your qualifications for the job you are seeking, and they want to see you in your best light. Remember, they must interview all candidates and a non-cooperative candidate may become a failure in spite of their best efforts to bring out his qualifications. Here are 15 suggestions that will help you:

1) Be natural – Keep your attitude confident, not cocky

If you are not confident that you can do the job, do not expect the board to be. Do not apologize for your weaknesses, try to bring out your strong points. The board is interested in a positive, not negative, presentation. Cockiness will antagonize any board member and make him wonder if you are covering up a weakness by a false show of strength.

2) Get comfortable, but don't lounge or sprawl

Sit erectly but not stiffly. A careless posture may lead the board to conclude that you are careless in other things, or at least that you are not impressed by the importance of the occasion. Either conclusion is natural, even if incorrect. Do not fuss with your clothing, a pencil or an ashtray. Your hands may occasionally be useful to emphasize a point; do not let them become a point of distraction.

3) Do not wisecrack or make small talk

This is a serious situation, and your attitude should show that you consider it as such. Further, the time of the board is limited – they do not want to waste it, and neither should you.

4) Do not exaggerate your experience or abilities

In the first place, from information in the application or other interviews and sources, the board may know more about you than you think. Secondly, you probably will not get away with it. An experienced board is rather adept at spotting such a situation, so do not take the chance.

5) If you know a board member, do not make a point of it, yet do not hide it

Certainly you are not fooling him, and probably not the other members of the board. Do not try to take advantage of your acquaintanceship – it will probably do you little good.

6) Do not dominate the interview

Let the board do that. They will give you the clues – do not assume that you have to do all the talking. Realize that the board has a number of questions to ask you, and do not try to take up all the interview time by showing off your extensive knowledge of the answer to the first one.

7) Be attentive

You only have 20 minutes or so, and you should keep your attention at its sharpest throughout. When a member is addressing a problem or question to you, give him your undivided attention. Address your reply principally to him, but do not exclude the other board members.

8) Do not interrupt

A board member may be stating a problem for you to analyze. He will ask you a question when the time comes. Let him state the problem, and wait for the question.

9) Make sure you understand the question

Do not try to answer until you are sure what the question is. If it is not clear, restate it in your own words or ask the board member to clarify it for you. However, do not haggle about minor elements.

10) Reply promptly but not hastily

A common entry on oral board rating sheets is "candidate responded readily," or "candidate hesitated in replies." Respond as promptly and quickly as you can, but do not jump to a hasty, ill-considered answer.

11) Do not be peremptory in your answers

A brief answer is proper – but do not fire your answer back. That is a losing game from your point of view. The board member can probably ask questions much faster than you can answer them.

12) Do not try to create the answer you think the board member wants

He is interested in what kind of mind you have and how it works – not in playing games. Furthermore, he can usually spot this practice and will actually grade you down on it.

13) Do not switch sides in your reply merely to agree with a board member

Frequently, a member will take a contrary position merely to draw you out and to see if you are willing and able to defend your point of view. Do not start a debate, yet do not surrender a good position. If a position is worth taking, it is worth defending.

14) Do not be afraid to admit an error in judgment if you are shown to be wrong

The board knows that you are forced to reply without any opportunity for careful consideration. Your answer may be demonstrably wrong. If so, admit it and get on with the interview.

15) Do not dwell at length on your present job

The opening question may relate to your present assignment. Answer the question but do not go into an extended discussion. You are being examined for a *new* job, not your present one. As a matter of fact, try to phrase ALL your answers in terms of the job for which you are being examined.

Basis of Rating

Probably you will forget most of these "do's" and "don'ts" when you walk into the oral interview room. Even remembering them all will not ensure you a passing grade. Perhaps you did not have the qualifications in the first place. But remembering them will help you to put your best foot forward, without treading on the toes of the board members.

Rumor and popular opinion to the contrary notwithstanding, an oral board wants you to make the best appearance possible. They know you are under pressure – but they also want to see how you respond to it as a guide to what your reaction would be under the pressures of the job you seek. They will be influenced by the degree of poise you display, the personal traits you show and the manner in which you respond.

ABOUT THIS BOOK

This book contains tests divided into Examination Sections. Go through each test, answering every question in the margin. We have also attached a sample answer sheet at the back of the book that can be removed and used. At the end of each test look at the answer key and check your answers. On the ones you got wrong, look at the right answer choice and learn. Do not fill in the answers first. Do not memorize the questions and answers, but understand the answer and principles involved. On your test, the questions will likely be different from the samples. Questions are changed and new ones added. If you understand these past questions you should have success with any changes that arise. Tests may consist of several types of questions. We have additional books on each subject should more study be advisable or necessary for you. Finally, the more you study, the better prepared you will be. This book is intended to be the last thing you study before you walk into the examination room. Prior study of relevant texts is also recommended. NLC publishes some of these in our Fundamental Series. Knowledge and good sense are important factors in passing your exam. Good luck also helps. So now study this Passbook, absorb the material contained within and take that knowledge into the examination. Then do your best to pass that exam.

EXAMINATION SECTION

EXAMINATION SECTION
TEST 1

DIRECTIONS: Each question or incomplete statement is followed by several suggested answers or completions. Select the one that BEST answers the question or completes the statement. *PRINT THE LETTER OF THE CORRECT ANSWER IN THE SPACE AT THE RIGHT.*

1. An employee under your supervision complains that he is assigned to work late more often than any of the other employees in the garage. You check the records and find that this isn't so.
   You should

   A. advise this employee not to worry about what the other employees do but to see that he puts in a full day's work himself
   B. explain to this employee that you get the same complaint from all the other employees
   C. inform this employee that you have checked the records and the complaint is not justified
   D. not assign this employee to work late for a few days in order to keep him satisfied

   1.____

2. A garage employee has reported late for work several times.
   His supervisor should

   A. give this employee less desirable assignments
   B. overlook the lateness if the employee's work is otherwise exceptional
   C. recommend disciplinary action for habitual lateness
   D. talk the matter over with the employee before doing anything further

   2.____

3. In choosing a man to be in charge in his absence, the supervisor should select first the employee who

   A. has ability to supervise others
   B. has been longest with the organization
   C. has the nicest appearance and manner
   D. is most skilled in his assigned duties

   3.____

4. An employee under your supervision comes to you to complain about a decision you have made In assigning the men. He is excited and angry. You think what he is complaining about is not important, but it seems very important to him.
   The BEST way for you to handle this is to

   A. let him talk until *he gets it off his chest* and then explain the reasons for your decision
   B. refuse to talk to him until he has cooled off
   C. show him at once how unimportant the matter is and how ridiculous his arguments are
   D. tell him to take it up with your superior if he disagrees with your decision

   4.____

5. Suppose that a new employee has been appointed and assigned to your supervision. When this man reports for work, it would be BEST for you to

   5.____

A. ask him questions about different problems connected with a motor vehicle and see if he answers them correctly
B. check him carefully while he carries out some routine assignment that you give him
C. explain to him the general nature of the work he will be required to do
D. make a careful study of his previous work record before coming to the Department

6. The competent supervisor will be friendly with the employees under his supervision but will avoid close familiarity.
This statement is justified MAINLY because

   A. a friendly attitude on the part of the supervisor toward the employee is likely to cause suspicion on the part of the employee
   B. a supervisor can handle his employees better if he doesn't know their personal problems
   C. close familiarity may interfere with the discipline needed for good supervisor-subordinate relationships
   D. familiarity with the employees may be a sign of lack of ability on the part of the supervisor

7. An employee disagrees with the instructions that you, his supervisor, have given him for carrying out a certain assignment.
The BEST action for you to take is to tell this employee that

   A. he can do what he wants but you will hold him responsible for failure
   B. orders must be carried out or morale will fall apart
   C. this job has been done in this way for many years with great success
   D. you will be glad to listen to his objections and to his suggestions for improvement

8. As a supervisor, it is LEAST important for you to use a new employee's probationary period for the purpose of

   A. carefully checking how he performs the work you assign him
   B. determining whether he can perform the duties of his job efficiently
   C. preparing him for promotion to a higher position
   D. showing him how to carry out his assigned duties properly

9. Suppose you have just given an employee under your supervision instructions on how to carry out a certain assignment.
The BEST way to check that he has understood your instructions is to

   A. ask him to repeat your instructions word for word
   B. check the progress of his work the first chance you get
   C. invite him to ask questions if he has any doubts
   D. question him briefly about the main points of the assignment

10. Suppose you find it necessary to change a procedure that the men under your supervision have been following for a long time.
A good way to get their cooperation for this change would be to

   A. bring them together to talk over the new procedure and explain the reasons for its adoption
   B. explain to the men that if most of them still don't approve of the change after giving it a fair try, you will consider giving it up

C. give them a few weeks' notice of the proposed change in procedure
D. not enforce the new procedure strictly at the beginning

11. An order can be given by a supervisor in such a way as to make the employee want to obey it.
According to this statement, it is MOST reasonable to suppose that

    A. a person will be glad to obey an order if he realizes that he must
    B. if an order is given properly, it will be obeyed more willingly
    C. it is easier to obey an order than to give one correctly
    D. supervisors should inspire confidence by their actions as well as by their words

12. If one of the men you supervise disagrees with how you rate his work, the BEST way for you to handle this is to

    A. advise him to appeal to your superior about it
    B. decline to discuss the matter with him in order to keep discipline
    C. explain why you rate him the way you do and talk it over with him
    D. tell him that you are better qualified to rate his work than he is

13. A supervisor should be familiar with the experience and abilities of the employees under his supervision MAINLY because

    A. each employee's work is highly important and requires a person of outstanding ability
    B. it will help him to know which employees are best fitted for certain assignments
    C. nearly all men have the same basic ability to do any job equally well
    D. superior background shortly shows itself in superior work quality, regardless of assignment

14. The competent supervisor will try to develop respect rather than fear in his subordinates.
This statement is justified MAINLY because

    A. fear is always present and, for best results, respect must be developed to offset it
    B. it is generally easier to develop respect in the men than it is to develop fear
    C. men who respect their supervisor are more likely to give more than the required minimum amount and quality of work
    D. respect is based on the individual and fear is based on the organization as a whole

15. If one of the employees you supervise does outstanding work, you should

    A. explain to him how his work can still be improved so that he will not become self-satisfied
    B. mildly criticize the other men for not doing as good a job as this man
    C. praise him for his work so that he will know it is appreciated
    D. say nothing or he might become conceited

16. A supervisor can BEST help establish good morale among his employees if he

    A. confides in them about his personal problems in order to encourage them to confide in him
    B. encourages them to become friendly with him but discourages social engagements with them

C. points out to them the advantages of having a cooperative spirit in the department
D. sticks to the same rules that he expects them to follow

17. The one of the following situations which would seem to indicate poor scheduling of work by the supervisor in a garage is

    A. everybody in the garage seeming to be very busy at the same time
    B. re-assignment of a man to other work because of breakdown of a piece of equipment
    C. two employees on vacation at the same time
    D. two operators waiting to have their vehicles greased and the oil changed

17.____

Questions 18-20.

DIRECTIONS: Questions 18 through 20 are to be answered ONLY on the basis of the information given in the following paragraph.

The supervisor will gain the respect of the members of his staff and increase his influence over them by controlling his temper and avoiding criticizing anyone publicly. When a mistake is made, the good supervisor will talk it over with the employee quietly and privately. The supervisor will listen to the employee's story, suggest the better way of doing the job, and offer help so the mistake won't happen again. Before closing the discussion, the supervisor should try to find something good to say about other parts of the employee's work. Some praise and appreciation, along with instruction, is more likely to encourage an employee to improve in those areas where he is weakest.

18. A good title that would show the meaning of this entire paragraph would be

    A. How to Correct Employee Errors
    B. How to Praise Employees
    C. Mistakes are Preventable
    D. The Weak Employe

18.____

19. According to the above paragraph, the work of an employee who has made a mistake is more likely to improve if the supervisor

    A. avoids criticizing him
    B. gives him a chance to suggest a better way of doing the work
    C. listens to the employee's excuses to see if he is right
    D. praises good work at the same time he corrects the mistake

19.____

20. According to the above paragraph, when a supervisor needs to correct an employee's mistake, it is important that he

    A. allow some time to go by after the mistake is made
    B. do so when other employees are not present
    C. show his influence with his tone of voice
    D. tell other employees to avoid the same mistake

20.____

Questions 21-24.

DIRECTIONS: Questions 21 through 24 are to be answered ONLY on the basis of the information given in the following paragraph.

All automotive accidents, no matter how slight, are to be reported to the Safety Division by the employee involved on Accident Report Form S-23 in duplicate. When the accident is of such a nature that it requires the filling out of the State Motor Vehicle Report Form MV-104, this form is also prepared by the employee in duplicate and sent to the Safety Division for comparison with the Form S-23. The Safety Division forwards both copies of Form MV-104 to the Corporation Counsel, who sends one copy to the State Bureau of Motor Vehicles. When the information on the Form S-23 indicates that the employee may be at fault, an investigation is made by the Safety Division. If this investigation shows that the employee was at fault, the employee's dispatcher is asked to file a complaint on Form D-11. The foreman of mechanics prepares a damage report on Form D-8 and an estimate of the cost of repairs on Form D-9. The dispatcher's complaint, the damage report, the repair estimate, and the employee's previous accident record are sent to the Safety Division where they are studied together with the accident report. The Safety Division then recommends whether or not disciplinary action should be taken against the employee.

21. According to the above paragraph, the Safety Division should be notified whenever an automotive accident has occurred by means of 21.____

    A. Form S-23
    B. Forms S-23 and MV-104
    C. Forms S-23, MV-104, D-8, D-9, and D-11
    D. Forms S-23, MV-104, D-8, D-9, and D-11 and employee's accident report

22. According to the above paragraph, the forwarding of the Form MV-104 to the State Bureau of Motor Vehicles is done by the 22.____

    A. Corporation Counsel
    B. dispatcher
    C. employee involved in the accident
    D. Safety Division

23. According to the above paragraph, the Safety Division investigates an automotive accident if the 23.____

    A. accident is serious enough to be reported to the State Bureau of Motor Vehicles
    B. dispatcher files a complaint
    C. employee appears to have been at fault
    D. employee's previous accident report is poor

24. Of the forms mentioned in the above paragraph, the dispatcher is responsible for preparing the 24.____

    A. accident report form
    B. complaint form
    C. damage report
    D. estimate of cost of repairs

Questions 25-27.

DIRECTIONS: Questions 25 through 27 are to be answered ONLY on the basis of the information given in the following paragraph.

One of the major problems in the control of city motor equipment, and especially passenger equipment, is keeping the equipment working for the city and for the city alone for as many hours of the day as is practical. Even when most city employees try to get the most out of the cars, a poor system of control will result in wasted car hours. Some city employees have a legitimate use for a car all day long while others use a car only a small part of the day and then let it stand. As a rule, trucks are easier to control than passenger cars because they are usually assigned to a specific job where a foreman continually oversees them. Even though trucks are usually fully utilized, there are times when the normal work assignment cannot be carried out because of weather conditions or seasonal changes. At such times, a control system could plan to make the trucks available for other uses.

25. According to the above paragraph, a problem connected with controlling the use of city motor equipment is 25.____

    A. increasing the life span of the equipment
    B. keeping the equipment working all hours of the day
    C. preventing the over-use of the equipment to avoid breakdowns
    D. preventing the private use of the equipment

26. According to the above paragraph, a good control system for passenger equipment will MOST likely lead to 26.____

    A. better employees being assigned to operate the cars
    B. fewer city employees using city cars
    C. fewer wasted car hours for city cars
    D. insuring that city cars are used for legitimate purposes

27. According to the above paragraph, a control system for trucks is useful because 27.____

    A. a foreman usually supervises each job
    B. special conditions sometimes prevent the planned use of a truck
    C. trucks are easier to control than passenger cars
    D. trucks are usually assigned to specific jobs where they cannot be fully utilized

Questions 28-33.

DIRECTIONS: In the paragraph below, some of the underlined words have been purposely changed and spoil the meaning that the rest of the paragraph is meant to give. Read the paragraph carefully, then answer Questions 28 through 33.

The motor vehicle supervisor who is <u>responsible</u> for training drivers in the operation of <u>special</u> equipment cannot expect a man to carry out all of his duties <u>poorly</u> <u>immediately</u> after receiving instruction. The employee may be <u>overwhelmed</u> by all of the details he must master, <u>happy</u> because he is <u>associated</u> with new fellow workers, or fearful that he may not <u>succeed</u> on the job. It is the supervisor's <u>job</u> to make the <u>operator</u> feel at ease and <u>discourage</u> his self-confidence. The supervisor must also vary the speed of the <u>driving</u> according to the operator's <u>capacity</u> to <u>absorb</u> the instruction without undue <u>pressure</u> or confusion. All learners <u>progress</u> through <u>several</u> stages of <u>development</u> <u>unless</u> they become expert in their duties. As the operator's skills <u>increase</u>, he will require <u>more</u> instruction but the supervisor should be available to correct <u>mistakes</u> promptly to prevent wrong <u>habits</u> being formed.

28. Of the following words underlined in the above paragraph, the one that does NOT give the real meaning that the rest of the paragraph is meant to give is

    A. responsible
    B. special
    C. happy
    D. immediately

29. Of the following words underlined in the above paragraph, the one that does NOT give the real meaning that the rest of the paragraph is meant to give is

    A. overwhelmed
    B. happy
    C. associated
    D. succeed

30. Of the following words underlined in the above paragraph, the one that does NOT give the real meaning that the rest of the paragraph is meant to give is

    A. job
    B. operator
    C. discourage
    D. self-confidence

31. Of the following words underlined in the above paragraph, the one that does NOT give the real meaning that the rest of the paragraph is meant to give is

    A. driving   B. capacity   C. absorb   D. pressure

32. Of the following words underlined in the above paragraph, the one that does NOT give the real meaning that the rest of the paragraph is meant to give is

    A. progress
    B. several
    C. development
    D. unless

33. Of the following words underlined in the above paragraph, the one that does NOT give the real meaning that the rest of the paragraph is meant to give is

    A. increase   B. more   C. mistakes   D. habits

Questions 34-40.

DIRECTIONS: Each of Questions 34 through 40 consists of a word in capital letters followed by four suggested meanings of the word. Select the word or phrase which means MOST NEARLY the same as the word in capital letters.

34. ACCELERATE

    A. adjust   B. press   C. quicken   D. strip

35. ALIGN

    A. bring into line
    B. carry out
    C. happen by chance
    D. join together

36. CONTRACTION

    A. agreement
    B. denial
    C. presentation
    D. shrinkage

37. INTERVAL

    A. ending
    B. mixing together of
    C. space of time
    D. weaken

38. LUBRICATE

    A. bend back   B. make slippery
    C. rub out   D. soften

39. OBSOLETE

    A. broken-down   B. hard to find
    C. high-priced   D. out of date

40. RETARD

    A. delay   B. flatten   C. rest   D. tally

KEY (CORRECT ANSWERS)

1.	C	11.	B	21.	A	31.	A
2.	D	12.	C	22.	A	32.	D
3.	A	13.	B	23.	C	33.	B
4.	A	14.	C	24.	B	34.	C
5.	C	15.	C	25.	D	35.	A
6.	C	16.	D	26.	C	36.	D
7.	D	17.	D	27.	B	37.	C
8.	C	18.	A	28.	C	38.	B
9.	D	19.	D	29.	B	39.	D
10.	A	20.	B	30.	C	40.	A

TEST 2

DIRECTIONS: Each question or incomplete statement is followed by several suggested answers or completions. Select the one that BEST answers the question or completes the statement. *PRINT THE LETTER OF THE CORRECT ANSWER IN THE SPACE AT THE RIGHT.*

Questions 1-3.

DIRECTIONS: Questions 1 through 3 consist of a word in capital letters followed by four suggested meanings of the word. Select the word or phrase which means MOST NEARLY the same as the word in capital letters.

1. SYNCHRONIZE

   A. draw out
   B. happen at the same time
   C. move at a steady rate
   D. turn smoothly

2. OSCILLATE

   A. attract   B. echo   C. roll   D. swing

3. TERMINAL

   A. last   B. moldy   C. named   D. spoken

4. In a certain garage, when the dispatcher issues gas and oil to a vehicle, he notes on his record the mileage reading of the vehicle.
   This is probably done MAINLY in order to

   A. check gas consumption against distance traveled
   B. compare age of vehicle with economy of operation
   C. decide when the vehicle should be scheduled for a grease job
   D. estimate future life expectancy of the vehicle

5. A supervisor of motor vehicle equipment was asked by the head of the bureau to investigate a certain procedure used in the garage and write a report with a recommendation whether the procedure should be changed. The supervisor, after he finished his investigation, made his report in which he said: *I recommend that you base your decision to change the present procedure on whether or not the new procedure will improve operations.*
   In this case, the supervisor carried out his assignment

   A. *poorly,* because he should have given his recommendation right at the beginning of the report
   B. *poorly,* because his investigation should have brought out whether the new procedure would improve operations
   C. *well,* because he left the final decision about changing the procedure up to the head of the bureau
   D. *well,* because he made an investigation and turned in a report as required

6. When a supervisor writes a report, it is LEAST important that

    A. all paragraphs in the report be of the same length
    B. a summary or list of the recommendations be given at the beginning of the report if the report is long
    C. independent ideas be taken up in separate paragraphs of the report
    D. the report give all the evidence on which the conclusions are based

7. The supervisor who makes a special point of using long words in preparing written reports is, in general, PROBABLY being

    A. *unwise,* because a written report should be factual and accurate
    B. *unwise,* because simplicity in a report is usually desirable
    C. *wise,* because the written report will become a permanent record
    D. *wise,* because with long words he can use the right emphasis in his report

8. The most thorough investigation is of no value if the report written by the person who made the investigation does not help his superior to decide what action to take.
According to this statement, it is LEAST correct to suppose that

    A. an investigation is of no value unless it is thorough
    B. a purpose of the report turned in after an investigation is to help supervisors decide what action to take
    C. the report on an investigation is usually written by the person who made the investigation
    D. the value of an investigation depends in part on the report turned in

9. Before you turn in a report you have written of an investigation that you made, you discover some additional information that you didn't know about before.
Whether or not you rewrite your report to include this additional information should depend MAINLY on the

    A. amount of time left in which to submit the report
    B. effect this information will have on the conclusions of the report
    C. number of changes that you will have to make in your original report
    D. possibility of turning in a supplementary report later

10. The advantage of using an *inspection check sheet* when making inspections of premises or equipment is that

    A. fewer inspections are required
    B. the inspection becomes easy and can be done by a subordinate
    C. there is less chance of forgetting some important point of the inspection
    D. there is less paper work

11. Of the following methods for keeping supplies and records of supplies, the one that will MOST quickly tell you at any time how many pieces of any item are on hand in the supply room is

    A. keeping a minimum number of each item on hand
    B. recording each item when it is added to or removed from stock
    C. stocking the same number of pieces of each item and reordering weekly to keep the count even
    D. taking a daily count

12. When a supervisor submits a report on a motor vehicle accident, it is LEAST important for him to include in his report the

    A. addresses of the witnesses to the accident
    B. number of the police precinct where the accident happened
    C. probable cause of the accident
    D. time of the accident

13. The MAIN reason a supervisor in charge of motor vehicle equipment or personnel should make sure that his men obey the safety rules is that

    A. accident prevention is a new program and should be tried out
    B. every accident can be prevented
    C. other safety measures are not needed where safety rules are obeyed
    D. safety rules are based on proven methods of accident prevention

14. When he investigates an accident in which a city vehicle was involved, the MAIN object of the supervisor should be to

    A. complete the investigation as fast as possible
    B. determine if the city operator's record is so bad that he should be fired
    C. get all the facts to establish the cause of the accident
    D. try to establish that the other driver was at least equally to blame

15. If witnesses to an automobile accident are interviewed separately, they are more likely to give different versions of the circumstances of the accident than if they are interviewed together.
    According to this statement, it is MOST probable that

    A. a truer picture of the circumstances of an accident can be gotten by interviewing the witnesses together rather than separately
    B. a witness's impression of what he saw is influenced by the statement of the other witnesses as to what they saw
    C. people who see an accident as a group will agree about the details of the accident more than people who are not together when they see the accident
    D. witnesses are less likely to tell the truth when interviewed privately than when interviewed as a group

16. A thorough investigation should always be made of an accident in which a city vehicle is involved.
    The MAIN value of such an investigation is to

    A. discover any factors that contributed to the accident which may be corrected
    B. keep compensation claims down
    C. provide good records from which statistics can be developed
    D. show the operators that accidents are taken seriously, no matter how small

17. An accident has been described as *an unplanned event caused by an unsafe act or condition.*
    An example of an unsafe act, rather than of an unsafe condition, in a garage is

    A. blocked fire exits   B. defective tools or equipment
    C. horseplay or teasing   D. oil and grease on floors

18. Of the following rules, the one that is LEAST directly concerned with the prevention of accidents is:

    A. Check brake fluid before leaving garage
    B. Do not use garage equipment if safety devices do not work
    C. No smoking in garage
    D. Reports of time lost due to accident must be submitted in 5 days

19. Which of the following entries on a Department Accident Report Form is MAINLY for the purpose of showing what is being done so that this type of accident will not happen again?

    A. Describe accident, including vehicle or vehicles involved
    B. What are you doing to prevent similar accidents?
    C. Why did the unsafe condition exist?
    D. Why was the unsafe act committed?

20. With respect to motor vehicle accidents, it is necessary to report in duplicate to the Bureau of Motor Vehicles on its printed forms

    A. all accidents
    B. only those accidents in which someone is killed or injured
    C. only those accidents in which someone is killed or injured or there is property damage of more than $50
    D. only those accidents in which someone is killed or injured or there is property damage of more than $100

21. A section of a garage used for parking vehicle measures 162 1/2' x 25 3/4'.
    If each vehicle to be parked in this section requires, on the average, 84 sq.ft. of parking space, the MAXIMUM number of vehicles that can be parked in this section is CLOSEST to

    A. 50   B. 45   C. 40   D. 35

22. Each of the 23 vehicles in a garage uses an average of 114 gallons of gas every 4 weeks.
    If the motor vehicle dispatcher is required to re-order gas when the gas tank in the garage shows no more than a one week supply, he MUST re-order when the gas tank shows _____ gallons.

    A. 655   B. 705   C. 830   D. 960

23. An employee's annual salary is $45,800. His total and annual deductions are 22% for withholding tax, 8 1/2% for pension and social security, and $1,820 for health insurance. The take-home pay that this employee would get on the check he receives every other week is MOST NEARLY

    A. $577.10   B. $845.00   C. $1,154.20   D. $1,220.40

24. A vehicle which averages 14 1/2 miles to a gallon of gas uses a quart of oil for every 21 1/2 gallons of gas.
    If the vehicle traveled 19,952 miles in a year, its oil consumption for the year would be _____ quarts.

    A. 52   B. 56   C. 60   D. 64

25. Thirteen percent of all the vehicles in a certain garage are trucks.
If there are 26 trucks, then the number of vehicles of other types in this garage is

   A. 174 B. 200 C. 260 D. 338

26. Of 12 employees in a garage, four earn $3,500 a year, two earn $3,150 a year, one earns $4,550 a year, and the rest each earn $3,800 a year.
The average yearly salary of these employees is CLOSEST to

   A. $3,550 B. $3,650 C. $3,750 D. $3,850

27. A garage bin used for storing supplies and parts measures 1 yard x 2 yards x 7 feet.
The cubic volume of this bin is

   A. 5 1/3 cubic yards
   B. 16 cubic feet
   C. 63 cubic feet
   D. 126 cubic feet

28. A garage has a gas tank with a capacity of 1,300 gallons. If there are only 520 gallons of gas in the tank, then the tank is _____ full.

   A. 40% B. 33 1/3% C. 25% D. 16 3/4%

29. Of a specially selected group of vehicles, 1/5 are 6 months old, 2/5 are 12 months old, and 2/5 are 15 months old.
The average age of this group of vehicles is _____ months.

   A. 9 B. 10 C. 11 D. 12

30. A suggestion has been made that every vehicle have its gas tank filled and oil and water checked when it returns to the garage at the end of the day.
This suggestion is

   A. *good,* mainly because the gas pump can be kept locked the rest of the day
   B. *good,* mainly because vehicles will be ready to go out promptly the next day
   C. *poor,* mainly because it would take too long to fill each vehicle
   D. *poor,* mainly because not every vehicle will need gas, oil, and water

31. Brakes do not generally have to be adjusted until the clearance between the bottom of the brake pedal and the floorboard goes below _____ inch(es).

   A. 2-2 1/2 B. 1 1/2-2 C. 1-1 1/2 D. 1/2-1

32. *Play* in the steering wheel is generally NOT considered to be excessive until it reaches about _____ inch(es).

   A. 1/2 B. 1 C. 1 1/2 D. 2

33. If the oil pressure gauge in a sedan reads unduly high even after the engine is warmed up, the MOST probable reason is

   A. a low oil level in the crankcase
   B. an internal leak in the oil system
   C. an obstruction in the oil line
   D. too light an oil being used

34. In order to keep tire pressure at the level recommended by the manufacturer, the air pressure in the tires should be

    A. checked at the end of the day's driving
    B. checked in the morning, before the vehicle is driven
    C. lower in summer than in winter
    D. reduced before a long trip to leave room for expansion

35. When inspecting one of your vehicles, you notice excessive wear on the center of the tread of both front tires.
    This unusual wear is MOST likely caused by

    A. excessive toe-in of the front wheels
    B. over-inflation of the front tires
    C. too much camber of the front wheels
    D. under-inflation of the front tires

36. The level of the fluid in the battery should be _____ the top of the plates.

    A. barely covering   B. exactly even with
    C. well below   D. well over

37. A heavy layer of oil on the water in the radiator would MOST probably indicate a

    A. cracked block   B. dirty air cleaner
    C. loose hose connection   D. water pump leak

38. If a five gallon can of gasoline is spilled on the garage floor, the BEST action to take is to

    A. let the gasoline evaporate
    B. pour sand over the puddle of gasoline
    C. squirt a foam-producing fire extinguisher on the puddle
    D. use a hose to flush the gasoline away

39. Greasy rags and waste in a garage should be

    A. hung up on a line to air out
    B. put in boxes that will be emptied daily
    C. put in covered metal cans or barrels
    D. put in wire baskets outside the garage

40. Adjusting the carburetor to give a mixture that is richer in fuel is

    A. *good* practice in cold weather as it improves engine operation
    B. *good* practice in very hot weather as it prevents stalling
    C. *poor* practice as it increases the chance of vapor lock
    D. *poor* practice in stop-and-go city driving as it greatly increases gas consumption

KEY (CORRECT ANSWERS)

1. B	11. B	21. A	31. C
2. D	12. B	22. A	32. D
3. A	13. D	23. C	33. C
4. A	14. C	24. D	34. B
5. B	15. B	25. A	35. B
6. A	16. A	26. B	36. D
7. B	17. C	27. D	37. A
8. A	18. D	28. A	38. D
9. B	19. B	29. D	39. C
10. C	20. D	30. B	40. A

TEST 3

DIRECTIONS: Each question or incomplete statement is followed by several suggested answers or completions. Select the one that BEST answers the question or completes the statement. *PRINT THE LETTER OF THE CORRECT ANSWER IN THE SPACE AT THE RIGHT.*

Questions 1-10.

DIRECTIONS: Questions 1 through 10 are based on the information given in the map on page 2.

1. On pay day, you assign an operator to deliver paychecks by car to the four work crews assigned to street jobs in the area. He starts from the garage and is to return there when finished.
   The order of delivery that would take the operator over the shortest allowable route would be crew

   A. 1, 2, 3, 4   B. 2, 1, 4, 3
   C. 3, 2, 1, 4   D. 4, 3, 2, 1

   1._____

2. Work crew 4 will be finished with its job at 1 P.M. and has to be moved to a new work location at Fir Ave. and 5th St. Work crew 3 will be finished with its job at the same time and has to be moved to begin work on a new job at 6th St. and Elm Ave. The operator assigned to the truck is to start from and return to the garage.
   In order to get each of these crews to their new locations as soon as possible, the dispatcher should instruct the operator assigned to pick up crew

   A. 3 and drop them at their new location; then pick up crew 4 and drop them at their new location
   B. 4 and drop them at their new location; pick up crew 3 and drop them at their new location
   C. 3; pick up crew 4; drop off crew 3; drop off crew 4
   D. 4; pick up crew 3; drop off crew 3; drop off crew 4

   2._____

3. The shortest allowable route for driving from the repair shop to the garage is 2nd Street and

   A. Fir Ave.
   B. Gladiola Ave.
   C. Gladiola Ave., 3rd St., Fir Ave.
   D. Holly Ave., 1st St., Gladiola Ave.

   3._____

4. You have requests for the following pick-ups and deliveries: a record player and loudspeaker to be moved from the playground to the skating rink, a case of pictures to be taken from the museum to the high school, and a ticket box to be moved from the stadium to the skating rink.
   Using the shortest allowable route from the garage and back, the order in which these pick-ups and deliveries should be made with the LEAST number of stops is

   A. museum, high school, playground, skating rink, stadium
   B. museum, playground, high school, stadium, skating rink
   C. playground, skating rink, museum, high school, stadium
   D. stadium, skating rink, museum, high school, playground

   4._____

16

A ◯ indicates a street work crew.

A ✗ indicates a an entrance.

Arrows on streets indicate one-way and two-way streets.
No U turns are permitted.

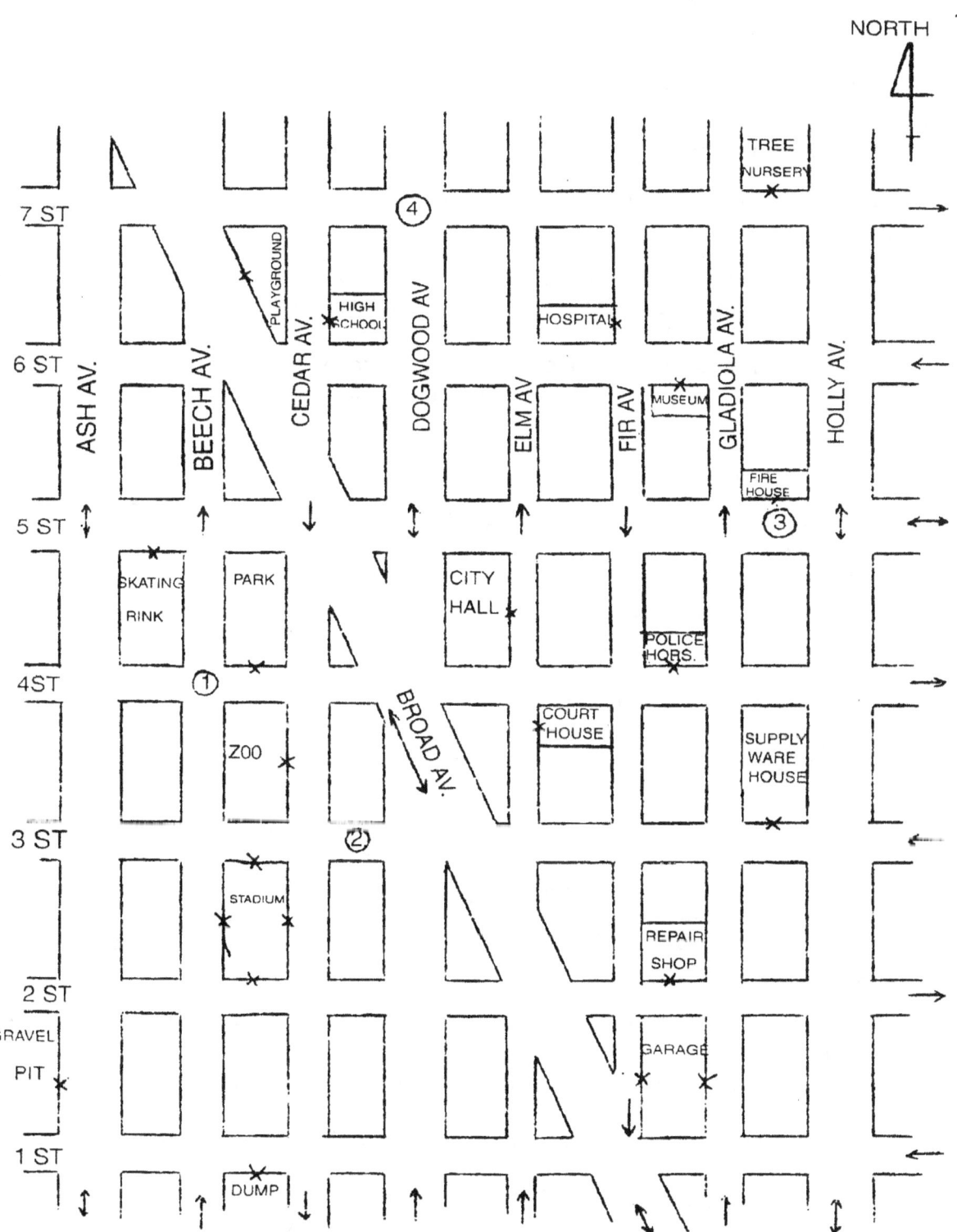

5. To help a newly assigned motor vehicle operator learn this area, you might ask him to study the direction of traffic patterns on the map.
It would be MOST helpful if you pointed out to him that two-way traffic is permitted on

   A. all but one of the numbered streets
   B. all but three of the named avenues
   C. only one of the numbered streets
   D. only three of the named avenues

6. In routing motor equipment to the northwestern part of the mapped area, the dispatcher would be wise to use Broad Avenue MAINLY because it is

   A. a two-way street
   B. a wide street
   C. near the garage
   D. the most direct route

7. A disadvantage of the construction and location of the repair shop, according to the map, is that

   A. it has only one entrance on 2nd St.
   B. it is located too close to the garage as equipment breakdowns would happen in the field
   C. motor equipment leaving the garage must go around the block to enter the shop
   D. the shop is too small in comparison to the size of the garage

8. Two factors about the construction and location of the garage that are of special advantage to the dispatcher are that it

   A. has two entrances and is near the repair shop
   B. has two entrances and one-way streets on all sides
   C. is near the repair shop and occupies a whole block
   D. occupies a whole block and has one-way streets on all sides

9. When dispatching equipment from the garage to the hospital, the dispatcher should use the entrance on

   A. either Gladiola Ave. or Fir Ave.
   B. Fir Ave.
   C. Gladiola Ave.
   D. 2nd St.

10. You have requests to pick up some small trees at the tree nursery to be delivered to the park, to pick up gravel at the gravel pit and deliver the load to the zoo, to take some broken benches from the park to the repair shop, to pick up supplies at the warehouse for delivery to City Hall and the court house.
The order in which a truck should do these jobs, starting from the garage and using the shortest allowable route is

   A. gravel pit, zoo; park, repair shop; warehouse, court house, City Hall; tree nursery, park, garage
   B. gravel pit, zoo; warehouse, court house, City Hall; tree nursery, park; park, repair shop; repair shop, garage
   C. tree nursery, park; park, repair shop; zoo, gravel pit; warehouse, court house, City Hall, garage
   D. warehouse, court house, City Hall; tree nursery, park; park, repair shop; gravel pit, zoo; zoo, garage

Questions 11-20.

DIRECTIONS: Answer Questions 11 through 20 ONLY on the basis of the information given below in the two charts and the Rules of the Department. You are to assume that you are the dispatcher in the garage where these charts are kept and where they are used in making daily assignments of operators and vehicles.

SECOND AVE. GARAGE MOTOR VEHICLE OPERATOR CONTROL SHEET Date: May 25, 19 __				SECOND AVE. GARAGE MOTOR VEHICLE OPERATOR CONTROL SHEET Date: May 25, 19 __			
Name of Operator	Cleared on	Hours of Overtime Credit as of May 25	On Vacation	Vehicle Number and Type	In Repair Shop as of May 25	Date Due in Shop for Preventive Maintenance Inspection	Date Last In Repair
Allen	P T	74		20-P		7/13	3/2
Boyd	P W	31	5/18-30	21-P		6/15	2/16
Cohen	P T	129		22-T		5/26	1/19
Diggs	P	15		23-P		6/1	5/8
Egan	P T	92	6/1-13	24-P		6/8	2/2
First	P T W	49		25-P		7/6	2/24
Gordon	P	57		26-W		6/1	1/21
Hanson	P T	143	6/15-27	27-T		7/20	4/6
				28-T	X	7/27	3/16
				29-P	X	5/18	1/12

Symbols: P - Passenger Car
T - Truck
W - Wrecker

Symbols: P - Passenger Car
T - Truck
W - Wrecker

RULES OF THE DEPARTMENT

1. A motor vehicle operator may be assigned to drive only those types of vehicles on which he has been cleared. No one but a motor vehicle operator may be assigned to drive a Department vehicle.

2. Private cars may not be used for Department business.

3. The motor vehicle dispatcher shall keep a daily record of overtime credits of all operators under his supervision to be sure that no operator acquires more than 150 hours of overtime credit. An assignment which involves overtime should be given, wherever possible, to the operator with the least overtime credit.

4. A vehicle due for preventive maintenance must be sent to the repair shop on the date it is due for preventive maintenance, except when a vehicle has been in the repair shop during the previous month.

5. All available vehicles are to be assigned to jobs as requested, with none held in reserve.

11. An official who is requesting a truck and operator for the three days beginning May 26th indicates to you that some overtime may be necessary for the operator, but he cannot predict how many hours of overtime will be needed. Under these circumstances, the MOST logical man for you to choose for this assignment would be operator

    A. Allen   B. Boyd   C. Diggs   D. First

12. The vehicle which does NOT have to be sent to the shop for preventive maintenance on the date it is due is vehicle number

    A. 23   B. 25   C. 27   D. 29

13. As dispatcher, you receive a request on May 25th for a truck and motor vehicle operator for a job that will take three days, from May 26th through May 28th.
    The vehicle that it would be BEST for you to choose on May 25th for this assignment is vehicle number

    A. 28   B. 27   C. 22   D. 20

14. On May 25th, right after all the vehicles have left the garage on daily assignment, you receive a call from your Commissioner's secretary. She tells you that an emergency has come up and asks you for a car to be ready in fifteen minutes to take a messenger with important papers to be delivered to the Commissioner who is waiting for the papers at a court in another borough.
    Of the following, the BEST thing for you to do, after explaining to the secretary that you have no cars available, is to

    A. advise her she should give you advance notice the next time so that you can reserve a car for the messenger
    B. offer to drive the messenger yourself in your private car
    C. promise to get a car from another department
    D. suggest that the messenger use public transportation

15. To give you more leeway in assigning your operators to the available equipment, it would be MOST practical for you to

    A. ask your supervisor to assign two additional motor vehicle operators to the garage
    B. have additional operators cleared on the wrecker
    C. suggest to your supervisor that rule 3 be abolished
    D. suggest to your supervisor that rule 1 be abolished

16. Other things being equal, the operator who should probably be of MOST value to you, as the dispatcher, is

    A. Cohen   B. Diggs   C. First   D. Hanson

17. The factor which indicates MOST strongly that there may not be enough operators assigned to this garage is the

    A. amount of overtime accumulated
    B. excess of number of vehicles over number of operators
    C. incomplete vacation schedule
    D. number of operators cleared on trucks

18. When dispatching men and equipment in the morning, it would be BEST for you to first dispatch men who   18.____

    A. are cleared on 1 vehicle
    B. are cleared on 2 vehicles
    C. are cleared on 3 vehicles
    D. have already had their vacations

19. The second week in June, you receive a call for an operator and wrecker.   19.____
    It is better to dispatch Boyd rather than First because

    A. he has already had his vacation
    B. he has less overtime
    C. he is not cleared on trucks
    D. unless there are special reasons, you might as well assign the men in alphabetical order for easier record keeping

20. You have requests for 6 passenger cars and 2 trucks for jobs on May 25th. All of these jobs will probably take the full day but none will require any overtime.   20.____
    How many of these requests for May 25th would you have to refuse?

    A. None   B. One
    C. Two   D. More than two

KEY (CORRECT ANSWERS)

1.	B	11.	D
2.	A	12.	A
3.	D	13.	B
4.	B	14.	D
5.	C	15.	B
6.	D	16.	C
7.	C	17.	A
8.	A	18.	A
9.	C	19.	C
10.	B	20.	B

TEST 4

DIRECTIONS: Each question or incomplete statement is followed by several suggested answers or completions. Select the one that BEST answers the question or completes the statement. *PRINT THE LETTER OF THE CORRECT ANSWER IN THE SPACE AT THE RIGHT.*

1. In a program of switching tires on a vehicle at regular intervals to give longer tire life, the BEST system to follow is

   A. [diagram]   B. [diagram]   C. [diagram]   D. [diagram]

   1._____

2. If an engine misfires when it is operated at low speed, the order in which the items below should be inspected, tested, and adjusted is

   A. breaker contact points, distributor cap and rotor, high voltage wires, spark plugs
   B. distributor cap and rotor, breaker contact points, spark plugs, high voltage wires
   C. high voltage wires, spark plugs, breaker contact points, distributor can and rotor
   D. spark plugs, high voltage wires, distributor cap and rotor, breaker contact points

   2._____

3. An operator complains that the headlights on his vehicle flare up and then dim as the speed of the vehicle changes.
   The MOST probable cause is

   A. a burned out fuse or defective circuit breaker
   B. a defective dimmer switch
   C. a loose connection in the headlight wiring
   D. weak bulbs

   3._____

4. A can of motor oil is marked *S.A.E. 20-20W.*
   This indicates that

   A. a mistake was made, and the oil should not be used
   B. chemicals have been added to winterize the oil
   C. the oil may be used both in medium temperatures and in winter weather
   D. the oil should be used when the temperature is between 20 degrees below and 20 degrees above zero

   4._____

5. A specific gravity reading of 1280 at 80° F means that a battery is

   A. fully discharged   B. nearing a discharged condition
   C. about half charged   D. fully charged

   5._____

6. If a generator constantly charges at a high rate, it is MOST probably due to a(n)

   A. defective regulator   B. dirty commutator
   C. too tight fan belt adjustment   D. overcharged battery

   6._____

7. In the servicing of spark plugs, it is IMPORTANT to

   A. bend the center electrode rather than the side electrode when adjusting the spark plug gap
   B. clean the spark plug recess in the cylinder head with a brush or compressed air after a spark plug has been removed
   C. make sure that each spark plug has only one gasket
   D. use an adjustable wrench to tighten a spark plug in its hole

8. If air gets into the lines of a hydraulic brake system, the MOST likely result will be

   A. a spongy pedal   B. grabbing brakes
   C. locked brakes   D. a hard pedal

9. In hooking test ammeters and voltmeters into a circuit, the ammeter

   A. should be connected in parallel and the voltmeter in series
   B. should be connected in series and the voltmeter in parallel
   C. and voltmeter should be connected in parallel
   D. and voltmeter should be connected in series

10. When brakes are correctly adjusted but one wheel takes hold before the others, it is MOST likely that the

    A. cup on the wheel cylinder has swelled
    B. relief port on the master cylinder isn't working
    C. push rod adjustment is faulty
    D. brake fluid has leaked into the lining

11. Racing an automobile engine on cold mornings to warm it up is

    A. *bad* practice, because there is poor lubrication of moving parts
    B. *good* practice, because the oil will reach moving parts faster
    C. *bad* practice, because it will form sludge in the engine
    D. *good* practice, because it will allow liquid gasoline to reach the crankcase

12. Using anti-freeze solution for more than a single season is

    A. *bad* practice, because it will cause excessive rust
    B. *good* practice, because it will be economical
    C. *bad* practice, because it will raise the boiling point
    D. *good* practice, because it will not clog the cooling system

13. The one of the following which is NOT usually a purpose of a preventive maintenance program for a fleet of automotive vehicles is

    A. a greater margin of safety in the operation of the vehicles
    B. easier and more comfortable driving
    C. improved mechanical ability of vehicle operators
    D. increased economy in vehicle operations

14. The one of the following which will NOT help improve gasoline mileage is

    A. driving at high speeds
    B. even acceleration
    C. keeping tires at recommended pressure
    D. using light oil in winter

15. An abnormally cool brake drum on one wheel after the vehicle has been in operation would MOST probably indicate a(n)

    A. dragging shoe
    B. improperly adjusted brake drum
    C. non-functioning brake
    D. underlubricated bearing

16. The pitman arm is part of the

    A. brake shoe assembly   B. driving axle
    C. fan belt assembly   D. steering mechanism

17. When he returns to the garage at the end of his shift, a motor vehicle operator complains to you that the engine *skips* on the car he is driving.
    When you prepare your requisition for a check-up of this vehicle, it is LEAST important for you to ask for a check of the

    A. battery   B. carburetor
    C. condenser   D. fuel line

18. In a garage where a vehicle preventive maintenance program is in operation, the one of the following which it is MOST important to do right away without waiting for next checkup is

    A. adjusting brakes that pull unevenly
    B. changing oil and lubrication to summer or winter grades
    C. checking spark plugs
    D. replacing an oil-soaked water hose

19. To test whether every cylinder has good compression, the instrument that should be used is a

    A. vacuum gauge   B. gas analyzer
    C. creeper   D. vent ball

20. It is generally recommended that the radiator of a passenger vehicle be flushed out

    A. every 1,000 miles   B. every fall and spring
    C. every 2,000 miles   D. once a year

KEY (CORRECT ANSWERS)

1. A
2. D
3. C
4. C
5. D

6. A
7. C
8. A
9. B
10. D

11. A
12. A
13. C
14. A
15. C

16. D
17. A
18. A
19. A
20. B

EXAMINATION SECTION
TEST 1

DIRECTIONS: Each question or incomplete statement is followed by several suggested answers or completions. Select the one that BEST answers the question or completes the statement. *PRINT THE LETTER OF THE CORRECT ANSWER IN THE SPACE AT THE RIGHT.*

1. Suppose that a new motor vehicle operator has been assigned to you, the dispatcher. It is your responsibility to see that he understands how to fill out the forms he is required to use.
   Of the following, the BEST way to do this would be to

   A. ask an experienced driver to tell him about the forms
   B. explain the purpose of each form to the new operator, and show him how to fill them out
   C. give the new man a copy of each form, so that he can study them
   D. tell the new man that filling out forms is simple, and that he should just follow the instructions on each form

   1.____

2. As a dispatcher, you may from time to time be faced with an important job problem.
   The usual way of solving a job problem includes the following four steps:
      I. Seeing what the facts mean in relation to the problem
      II. Choosing the best solution
      III. Getting all the important facts relating to the problem
      IV. Finding possible solutions
   If the above four numbered steps were arranged in the order in which they should be taken, the CORRECT order would be

   A. IV, III, I, II   B. IV, I, III, II
   C. III, I, IV, II   D. I, IV, III, II

   2.____

3. Of the following, it is LEAST desirable that a dispatcher

   A. correct a driver for a minor rule violation, even if it is the first time that the driver broke the rule and no harm was done
   B. discuss with any new drivers he supervises some situations that may come up in their work and how to handle them
   C. encourage the drivers he supervises to ask him questions about any of his instructions that they do not understand
   D. observe for a few days the mistakes one of his drivers makes and then discuss these mistakes with him

   3.____

4. Suppose you receive a telephone call from an employee who complains that, while being driven on official business, he was treated rudely by the driver.
   As the dispatcher who supervises this driver, which of the following actions should you take FIRST?

   A. Tell the caller that you will have the driver write him a letter of apology
   B. Tell the caller that you will have the driver telephone him to apologize
   C. Ask the other drivers you supervise if this driver is generally discourteous
   D. Try to get the details of the incident from the caller and from the driver

   4.____

5. When a certain dispatcher has to criticize one of his drivers, he makes a practice of doing it in private.
   This practice is GENERALLY

   A. *good;* private criticism can help save the driver unnecessary embarrassment
   B. *bad;* open criticism helps develop among the drivers a feeling of being treated fairly
   C. *good;* private criticism leaves no hard feelings between the driver and the dispatcher
   D. *bad;* open criticism keeps the drivers on their toes

6. A certain dispatcher often issues orders in the form of a request rather than in the form of a command.
   This is

   A. *good;* it lets the driver decide the best way to carry out such an order
   B. *poor;* it shows that the dispatcher lacks sufficient self-confidence
   C. *good;* it helps to create good will with the drivers
   D. *poor;* it puts the responsibility on the drivers to decide which job to do first

7. For a dispatcher to judge the performance of a driver exclusively on how well he drives, his safety record, and his neatness of appearance would be

   A. *undesirable;* there are other important factors to consider also
   B. *desirable;* these factors are objective and eliminate personal bias
   C. *undesirable;* these factors should have been judged before the driver was appointed
   D. *desirable;* this method stresses on-the-job performance

8. Suppose you discover that you have unfairly criticized one of the drivers you supervise.
   Of the following, the BEST thing for you to do would be to

   A. think of some indirect way to let the driver know you realize that he was not at fault
   B. admit your mistake to the driver, and apologize
   C. overlook some offense that the driver commits in the future
   D. make up for it by giving this driver better assignments for a short time

9. A driver, who otherwise does a rather good job, is starting to arrive late for work too often. You, as the dispatcher, have called him in to talk to him about it.
   Which of the following would be BEST for you to do?

   A. Let him know right away that there are no excuses for being late this much
   B. Discuss these latenesses with him but also mention good points in his work
   C. Give him a strong warning of punishment in order to stop the habit right away
   D. Tell him that he ought to improve to keep the other drivers from complaining

10. A year ago you corrected one of the men you supervise for driving carelessly while in the garage. Since then he has been careful not to repeat such actions.
    To remind this driver once in a while about that careless act would be

    A. *good;* it will help to keep him from doing it again
    B. *bad;* it suggests to this subordinate that you have a bad memory
    C. *good;* he will know that you have not forgotten an important infraction
    D. *bad;* the incident is over and he has not done anything like it since

11. Lately one of the drivers that you supervise has not been doing as good a job as he used to do. He asks whether he may discuss with you a problem that has been bothering him. He says he thinks that the problem has been affecting his work. But after he tells you the problem, you feel that this is really a minor problem and that he has somehow failed to consider certain alternatives open to him.
Of the following, the FIRST thing you should do is to

    A. examine with him possibilities for solving the problem
    B. tell him it is a minor problem
    C. tell him the solution to the problem
    D. explain to him that he must not let such problems disturb him in his work

11.____

12. Suppose that you, the dispatcher, instruct a motor vehicle operator to make a delivery and to use a certain route which you believe is the fastest and shortest. The driver then says that he knows a shorter, faster route.
Of the following, it would be BEST for you to

    A. tell the driver to follow your route and not question the orders of his supervisor
    B. assign this delivery to a driver who agrees that your route is best
    C. ask your supervisor to decide which is the best route so the driver will know that you are open-minded
    D. have the driver describe the other route and let him use it if it seems at least as good as yours

12.____

13. Your department has just made a major policy change affecting work procedures for the 30 men under your supervision, and they do not yet know about it. You wish to reduce or eliminate lasting negative reactions and to gain as much acceptance of this policy change as possible.
Which of the following is the BEST method to use to accomplish this purpose?

    A. Circulate a memo to them describing the policy change in detail
    B. Call a meeting with them to inform them thoroughly of the policy change, and to answer questions
    C. Make clear to the men that the policy change was not your idea, but that it must be followed
    D. Announce the policy change at a meeting and end the meeting before objections can be raised

13.____

14. A driver asks you, the dispatcher, about a suggestion he plans to send in to the employees' suggestion program. You doubt whether his suggestion can be used because you think it will be unacceptable to most employees; that they will resist its use.
Of the following, the BEST thing for you to do would be to tell him

    A. why you do not think he should send in the suggestion
    B. your doubts about the suggestion, but encourage him to send it in anyway
    C. that you think it is a good suggestion and that he should send it in
    D. not to send in the suggestion unless he can think of some way to get employees to accept it

14.____

15. A dispatcher should periodically check the procedures and practices in his garage to see whether any changes should be made.
Which of the following is the MAIN reason for checking in this manner?

15.____

A. All necessary changes in procedures can, in this way, be made immediately.
B. Frequent changes in procedures are welcomed by employees.
C. It is the dispatcher's responsibility to try to improve, when possible, the operations he supervises.
D. The dispatcher is fully responsible for deciding the important changes in procedure in his garage.

16. A driver has been transferred from another garage to the one in which you are the dispatcher. The driver's former supervisor calls to tell you that the driver is uncooperative. Of the following, the BEST thing for you to do would be to

    A. tell the driver that you are aware of the fact that he gave very little cooperation to the other dispatcher, but that you will treat him fairly
    B. test as soon as possible how much the driver is willing to cooperate
    C. wait to see how the driver reacts under your supervision
    D. make arrangements to have him transferred to another assignment

17. A driver accuses you, the dispatcher, of favoritism. For you to ask the driver to be more specific would be

    A. *bad;* it may create an argument with consequent bad feelings on both sides
    B. *good;* it can help in settling the matter
    C. *bad;* it puts the driver in a position where he will have to defend himself
    D. *good;* it shows the driver that you are fair

18. Which one of the following is LEAST likely to mean that your drivers like their jobs?

    A. Most of the drivers have excellent attendance reports.
    B. The drivers do their work to the best of their ability.
    C. The drivers admire and respect their supervisors.
    D. Most of the drivers have had at least some high school.

19. Of the following situations, which one would the dispatcher MOST likely be able to handle by himself without discussing it with his superior?

    A. A disagreement comes up between two of his drivers about the meaning of a departmental regulation.
    B. Additional drivers are needed because of a permanent increase in the work load.
    C. One of the drivers he supervises deliberately disregards his instructions, despite warnings and previous punishment for doing this.
    D. The drivers are complaining about the great amount of overtime work required.

20. A dispatcher and a few of his drivers are going to lift a heavy object together. The dispatcher tells the men not to lift until he gives a signal to begin lifting.
    Of the following, the BEST reason for these instructions is that they help

    A. alert the men to be careful not to hurt themselves when lifting
    B. get the men to lift with all their available strength
    C. maintain the dispatcher's position as the leader of the group
    D. avoid too much strain on any member of the group

KEY (CORRECT ANSWERS)

1.	B	11.	A
2.	C	12.	D
3.	D	13.	B
4.	D	14.	B
5.	A	15.	C
6.	C	16.	C
7.	A	17.	B
8.	B	18.	D
9.	B	19.	A
10.	D	20.	D

TEST 2

DIRECTIONS: Each question or incomplete statement is followed by several suggested answers or completions. Select the one that BEST answers the question or completes the statement. *PRINT THE LETTER OF THE CORRECT ANSWER IN THE SPACE AT THE RIGHT.*

1. The EASIEST and QUICKEST way of finding which spark plug is bad and causing an engine to miss is to

    A. remove each plug and examine it
    B. replace each plug, one at a time, with a new one
    C. check each plug with a timing light
    D. short circuit each plug, one at a time

    1._____

2. A pressure cap is used in an automotive cooling system to

    A. measure the water pressure
    B. prevent cold water from reaching the engine
    C. raise the boiling point of the water
    D. aid circulation of water in the cooling system

    2._____

3. The necessity to frequently add large amounts of water to a car storage battery is MOST likely an indication that the

    A. charging rate is too high
    B. charging rate is too low
    C. battery connection is loose
    D. ground connection is loose

    3._____

4. Inspection of an automobile tire shows that the center treads have had more wear than the side treads.
   The MOST common cause for this condition is

    A. too much camber   B. cornering
    C. overinflation   D. underinflation

    4._____

5. Graphite is a recommended lubricant for automotive

    A. springs   B. car door locks
    C. differentials   D. steering shafts

    5._____

6. The ignition coil on a gasoline engine

    A. transforms low voltage to high voltage
    B. prevents sparking at the breaker points
    C. limits charging voltage on the battery
    D. prevents excessive flow of current to the spark plugs

    6._____

7. The MAIN function of a thermostat in the radiator of an automobile is to

    A. prevent cold water from circulating between the engine and the radiator
    B. permit full flow of cooling water to the engine when starting the engine up
    C. prevent cooling water from overheating
    D. alert the driver that the engine is overheating

    7._____

8. The one of the following automotive components or systems that is NOT considered a part of the *power train* is the

   A. propeller shaft
   B. ignition system
   C. transmission
   D. clutch

9. Suppose in your garage records are kept of the vehicular accidents your men have while driving at work. In addition to the number of accidents each man has, which of the following facts in the records would be the MOST important for comparing drivers on their success in avoiding driving accidents while working?
The

   A. number of years of driving experience of each man
   B. number of miles driven by each driver on the job
   C. gasoline consumption of each vehicle
   D. age of the drivers assigned to the garage

10. A department has asked dispatchers to study the standard forms and reports they fill out each day, and to make recommendations for revision.
Which of the following is the BEST reason for a dispatcher to suggest that certain information no longer be asked on such forms?

    A. The information is no longer applicable to this department.
    B. Although the information is accurate, it becomes outdated after a while.
    C. The information is difficult to evaluate on the level of the dispatcher.
    D. The information requested can only be estimated at ninety-eight percent accuracy.

Questions 11-18.

DIRECTIONS: Questions 11 through 18 are to be answered according to the information given in the notes and map that appear on Page 3 following.

NOTES

A circle with a number inside (③) indicates a street work crew.

A cross (X) indicates an entrance and exit.

Arrows on streets indicate (→) one-way and (↔) two-way streets.

No U-turns are permitted.

Disregard the width of the streets, avenues, and boulevards in arriving at your answers.

Assume that for each standard block shown on the map, the length (from street to street) is twice as big as the width (from avenue to avenue).

3 (#2)

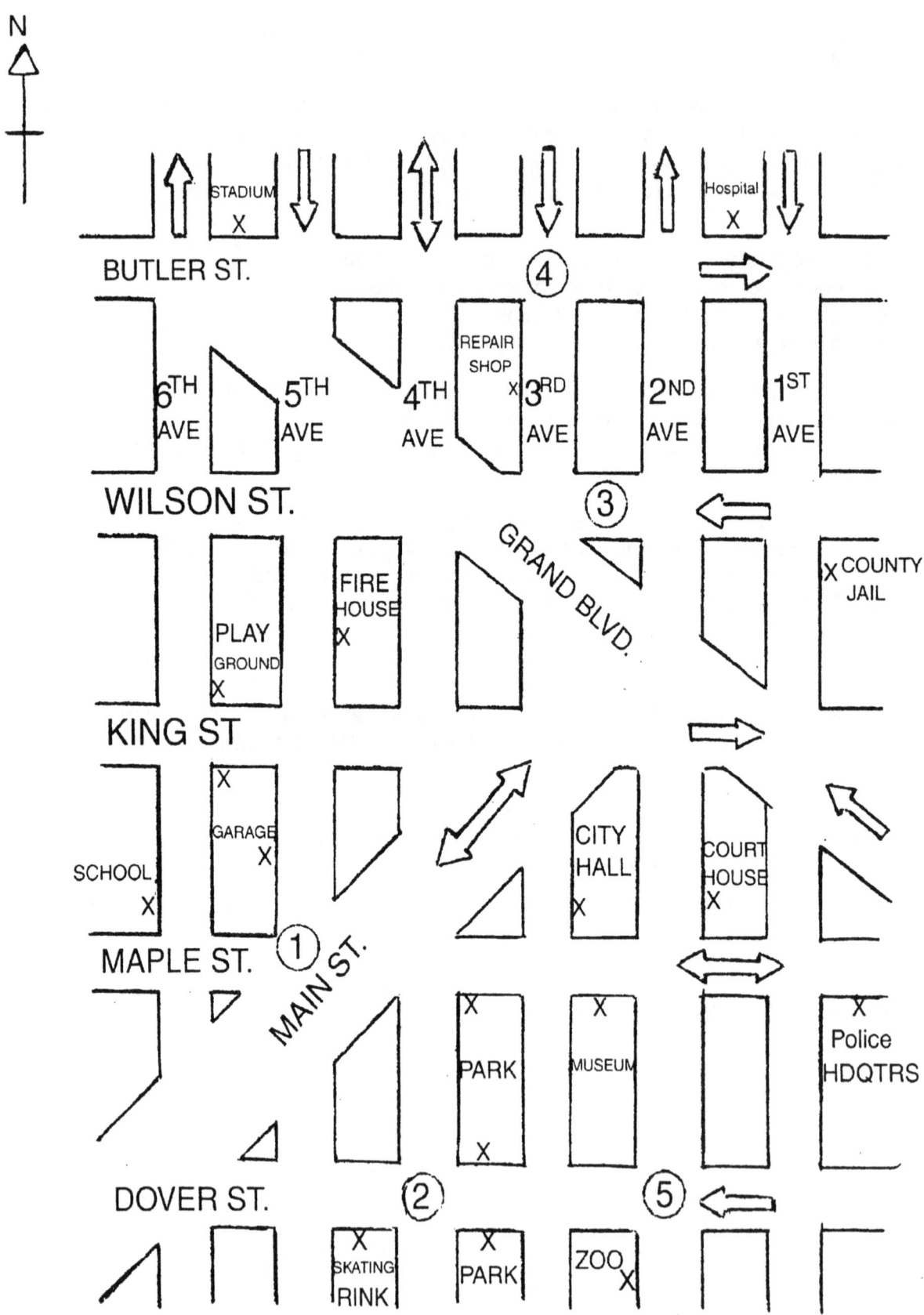

34

11. A driver should turn left when exiting from the 11.____

    A. court house B. playground
    C. stadium D. repair shop

12. An operator, facing west on Wilson St. and 2nd Ave., wants to drive to Dover St. and 6th 12.____
    Ave.
    The SHORTEST allowable route for him to take is

    A. Wilson St., 3rd Ave., and Main St.
    B. Wilson St., 5th Ave., and Dover St.
    C. Wilson St., 3rd Ave., Maple St., 5th Ave., and Dover St.
    D. 2nd Ave., Grand Blvd., and Main St.

13. The SHORTEST allowable route for driving from the repair shop exit to the garage 13.____
    entrance is to use Third Ave.,

    A. Maple St., and 6th Ave.
    B. and King St.
    C. Main St., and 5th Ave.
    D. Wilson St., and 5th Ave.

14. An emergency repair has to be made in front of the entrance to the fire house and a work 14.____
    crew is needed there immediately. The dispatcher is told to send the crew that can reach
    the fire house entrance first, using the shortest allowable driving distance.
    Which crew should he send?
    Crew

    A. 1 B. 2 C. 3 D. 4

15. Which describes BEST the location of the museum in relation to the school? 15.____
    The museum is located _____ of the school.

    A. southwest B. southeast C. northwest D. northeast

16. Work Crew 5 will be finished with its job at 1 P.M. and has to join Work Crew 3 for the rest 16.____
    of the day. Work Crew 4 will also be finished at 1 P.M. and must join Work Crew 2 for the
    rest of the day. The driver of the truck is to start from inside the garage, take Work Crews
    5 and 4 to their new locations, and return into the garage. Of the following choices, the
    driver will cover the SHORTEST allowable route if he picks up crew

    A. 5, drops off crew 5 at crew 3, picks up crew 4, drops off crew 4 at crew 2
    B. 4, picks up crew 5, drops off crew 5 at crew 3, drops off crew 4 at crew 2
    C. 4, drops off crew 4 at crew 2, picks up crew 5, drops off crew 5 at crew 3
    D. 5, picks up crew 4, drops off crew 5 at crew 3, drops off crew 4 at crew 2

17. One operator is assigned to pick up a city official at the hospital and drive him to the 17.____
    entrance to City Hall. The SHORTEST allowable route to take from the hospital is Butler
    St., First Ave.,

    A. Maple St., and Third Ave.
    B. Wilson St. 2nd Ave., Grand Blvd., Main St., and Third Ave.
    C. Maple St., Main St., and Third Ave.
    D. Wilson St., and Third Ave.

18. Of the following, which entrance is the SHORTEST allowable driving distance from the school exit?
    The entrance to

    A. the hospital
    B. police headquarters
    C. the County Jail
    D. the museum

Questions 19-20.

DIRECTIONS: A city vehicle has been involved in an accident and a diagram of the accident has been prepared. Answer Questions 19 and 20 according to the information given in the diagram and notes below.

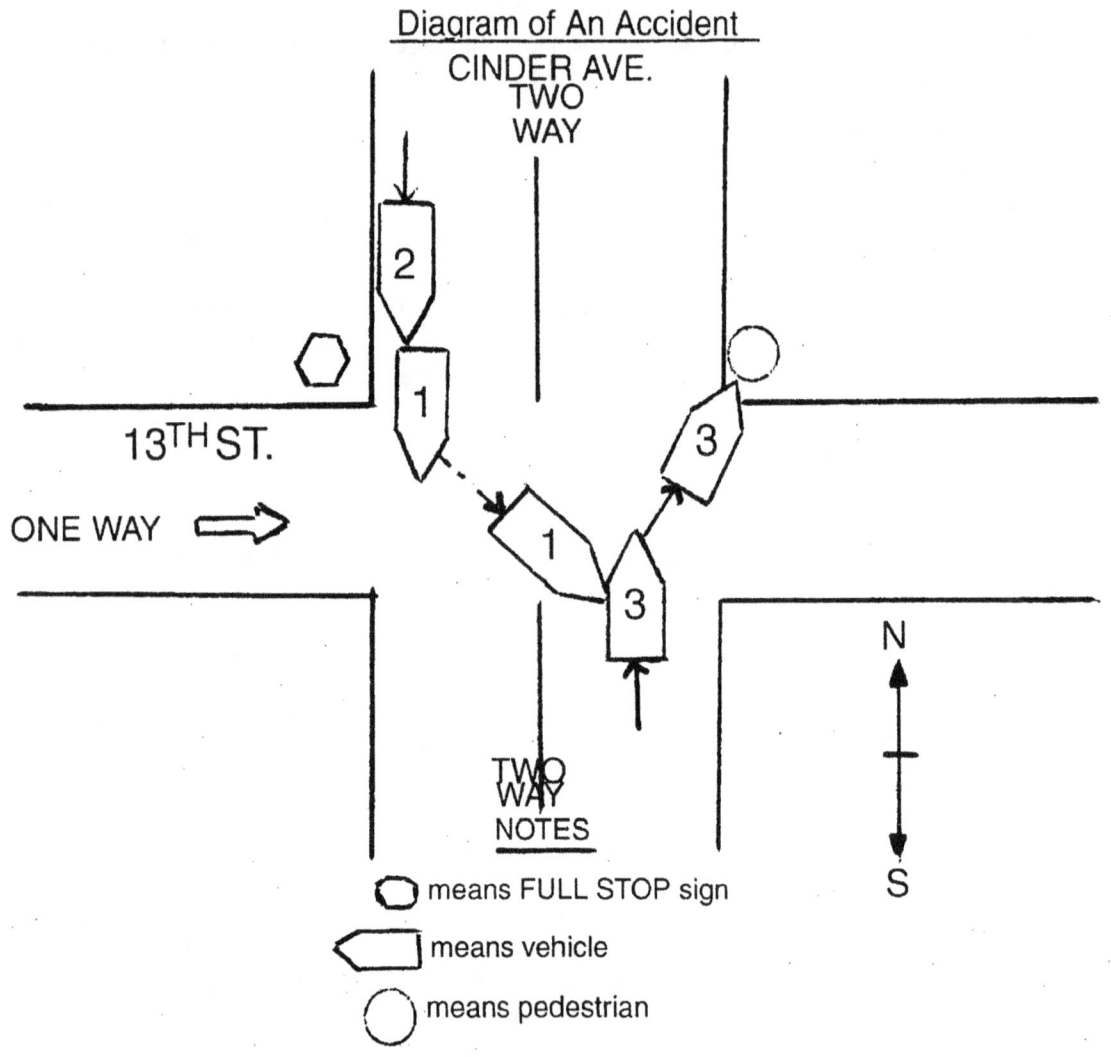

Solid arrow (←) means direction of travel before accident.

Broken arrow (←--) means direction of travel after accident. Vehicle #1 is the city vehicle.

19. The FULL STOP sign is located on the _____ corner of the intersection.

    A. northeast   B. northwest   C. southeast   D. southwest

20. If the driver of the city vehicle was following driving regulations, it is MOST likely that at the time he was hit he was 20._____

    A. making a right turn
    B. making a left turn
    C. standing still
    D. driving down Cinder Avenue

KEY (CORRECT ANSWERS)

1.	D	11.	C
2.	C	12.	A
3.	A	13.	D
4.	C	14.	C
5.	B	15.	B
6.	A	16.	A
7.	A	17.	D
8.	B	18.	D
9.	B	19.	B
10.	A	20.	D

TEST 3

DIRECTIONS: Each question or incomplete statement is followed by several suggested answers or completions. Select the one that BEST answers the question or completes the statement. *PRINT THE LETTER OF THE CORRECT ANSWER IN THE SPACE AT THE RIGHT.*

Questions 1-19.

DIRECTIONS: In each of Questions 1 through 19, choose the lettered word which means MOST NEARLY the same as the word in capital letters.

1. APPRAISE
   A. inform   B. evaluate   C. increase   D. decrease

2. IMPARTIAL
   A. strange   B. funny   C. fair   D. bad

3. INCENTIVE
   A. cash   B. fire   C. messenger   D. motive

4. INSUBORDINATE
   A. confusing   B. disobedient
   C. important   D. smart

5. NEGLIGENT
   A. careless   B. painful   C. cruel   D. untidy

6. REVISION
   A. change   B. decision   C. dream   D. retreat

7. SEMIANNUALLY
   A. four times in a year   B. three times in a year
   C. twice in a year   D. every other year

8. UTILIZE
   A. break   B. cook   C. reduce   D. use

9. VAGUE
   A. new   B. sure   C. old   D. uncertain

10. CENTRIFUGAL
    A. moving away from a center
    B. moving toward a center
    C. having a center
    D. without a center

11. INDUCE
    A. cause   B. stop   C. name   D. signal

12. PERTINENT
    A. wise
    C. relevant
    B. stormy
    D. understood

13. ENUMERATE
    A. free   B. count   C. postpone   D. obey

14. DEPLETE
    A. hide   B. order   C. purchase   D. empty

15. DIVERSE
    A. average   B. varied   C. faulty   D. hollow

16. MESH
    A. engage   B. skip   C. spin   D. use

17. DISMANTLE
    A. lock up
    C. look over
    B. forget about
    D. take apart

18. INCIDENTAL
    A. casual
    C. infrequent
    B. necessary
    D. needless

19. ELASTIC
    A. resilient
    C. tranquil
    B. reserved
    D. sterile

20. Truck A has been driven 38,742.3 miles, Truck B has been driven 24,169.7 miles, Truck C has been driven 41,286.4 miles, Truck D has been driven 15,053.5 miles, and Truck E has been driven 8,407.0 miles.
    The total mileage of these five trucks combined is MOST NEARLY _____ miles.
    A. 127,650   B. 127,660   C. 128,650   D. 128,660

21. Suppose that the trucks in a certain garage used a total of 86,314 gallons of gas in 1991 and 8,732 gallons less in 1992.
    If they used a total of 72,483 gallons of gas in 1993, how much LESS gas was used in 1993 than in 1992?
    _____ gallons.
    A. 5,099   B. 5,109   C. 5,199   D. 5,209

22. A driver averaged 17 miles for each gallon of gas used one week and 26 miles the next week.
    If he used 38.9 gallons during the first week and 27.6 during the second, the TOTAL number of miles he drove in these two weeks was _____ miles.

A. 1,266.3   B. 1,322.6   C. 1,378.9   D. 1,435.2

23. In Garage A, 87 drivers worked a total of 427 hours overtime. In Garage B, 53 drivers worked a total of 245 hours overtime.
Compared to the average overtime worked per man in Garage B, the average overtime worked per man in Garage A was MOST NEARLY _____ of an hour _____ .

    A. 2/10; more
    B. 2/10; less
    C. 3/10; more
    D. 3/10; less

24. The scale on a map indicates that every 1 5/8 inches on the map represents 5 miles. If two locations are 13 inches apart on the map, what is the distance between them, in miles?

    A. 30   B. 35   C. 40   D. 45

25. If a car is traveling on a highway at a steady speed of 35 miles an hour, how many miles will it go in a period of 24 minutes?
_____ miles.

    A. 13   B. 14   C. 15   D. 16

26. An employee's annual salary is $7,625.
If he receives a 5.4% salary increase, his new annual salary will be

    A. $7,992.50
    B. $8,036.75
    C. $8,147.25
    D. $8,169.00

27. Of the 60 drivers assigned to a garage, 1/6 of them live in County A, 1/4 of them live in County B, 1/5 of them live in County C, and the rest live in County D.
How many of the drivers live in County D?

    A. 22   B. 23   C. 24   D. 25

28. Driver Green travels 33 miles along express highways at an average speed of 44 miles an hour to get to his destination. Driver Smith travels 28 miles through traffic at an average speed of 21 miles an hour to get to the same destination.
If Mr. Smith starts his trip a half hour before Mr. Green, he will reach the destination _____ Mr. Green.

    A. 5 minutes before
    B. at the same time as
    C. 5 minutes after
    D. 10 minutes after

29. A 210 foot by 120 foot parking lot is reduced in size by construction of a 36 foot by 54 foot building at one of its corners.
The area left for parking is MOST NEARLY _____ square yards.

    A. 1,800   B. 2,600   C. 22,800   D. 23,300

30. A dispatcher works a total of 44 hours, spending 17 on Special Project A, 13 on Special Project B, and the rest on his usual duties.
The percentage of time he spends on the two special projects is MOST NEARLY

    A. 68%   B. 69%   C. 70%   D. 71%

31. A driver, dispatched from the garage at 8:15 A.M., arrived at his first destination 35 minutes later. He waited 50 minutes at this location before he could go on to his next destination. It took him one hour and 40 minutes traveling time to get to this second location. He then took an hour lunch period before driving back to the garage, a trip that took 45 minutes.
What time did the driver return to the garage?
_____ P.M.

   A. 12:25   B. 12:45   C. 1:05   D. 1:25

Questions 32-35.

DIRECTIONS: Questions 32 through 35 are to be answered according to the information given in the following passage.

ACCIDENT PRONENESS

Accident proneness is a subject deserving much more attention than it has received. Studies have shown a high incidence of accidents to be associated with particular employees who are called accident prone. Such employees, according to these studies, behave on their jobs in ways which make them likely to have more accidents than would normally be expected.

It is important to point out the difference between the employee who is a "repeater" and the one who is truly accident prone. It is obvious that any person assigned to work about which he knows little will be liable to injury until he does learn the "how" of the job. Few workers left completely on their own will develop adequate safe practices. Therefore, they must be trained. Only those who fail to respond to proper training should be regarded as accident prone.

The dangers of an occupation should also be considered when judging an accident record. For a crane operator, a record of five accidents in a given period of time may not indicate accident proneness, while, in the case of a clerk, two accidents over the same period of time may be excessive. There are the repeaters whose accident records can be explained by correctible physical defects, by correctible unsafe plant or machine conditions, or by assignment to work for which they are not suited because they cannot meet all the job's physical requirements. Such repeaters cannot be fairly called "accident prone." A diagnosis of accident proneness should not be lightly made, but should be based on all of these considerations.

32. According to the above passage, studies have shown that accident prone employees

   A. work under unsafe physical conditions
   B. act in unsafe ways on the job
   C. are not usually physically suited for their jobs
   D. work in the more dangerous occupations

33. According to the above passage, a person who is accident prone

   A. has received proper training which has not reduced his tendency toward accidents
   B. repeats the same accident several times over a short period of time
   C. experiences excessive anxiety about dangers in his occupation
   D. ignores unsafe but correctible machine conditions

34. According to the above passage, MOST persons who are given work they know little about

    A. will eventually learn on their own sufficient safety practices to follow
    B. work safely if they are not accident prone
    C. must be trained before they develop adequate safety methods
    D. should be regarded as accident prone until they become familiar with the job

35. According to the above passage, to effectively judge the accident record of an employee, one should consider

    A. the employee's age and physical condition
    B. that five accidents are excessive
    C. the type of dangers that are natural to his job
    D. the difficulty level of previous occupations held by the employee

Questions 36-39.

DIRECTIONS: Questions 36 through 39 are to be answered according to the information given in the following paragraph.

FIRES

The four types of fives are called Class A, Class B, Class C, and Class D. Examples of Class A fires are paper, cloth, or wood fires. The types of extinguishers used on Class A fires are foam, soda acid, or water. Class B fires are those in burning liquids. They require a smothering action for extinguishment. Carbon dioxide, dry chemical, vaporizing liquid, or foam are the types of extinguishers that are used on burning liquids. Electrical fires, such as in motors and switches, are Class C fires. A non-conducting extinguishing agent must be used for this kind of fire. Therefore, carbon dioxide, dry chemical, or vaporizing liquid extinguishers are used. Fires in motor vehicles are Class D fires, and carbon dioxide, dry chemical, or vaporizing liquid extinguishers should be used on them.

36. According to the information in the above paragraph, a fire in a can full of gasoline would be a Class _____ fire.

    A. D   B. C   C. B   D. A

37. In the above paragraph, the extinguishers recommended are entirely the same for Class _____ and Class _____ fires.

    A. B; D   B. C; D   C. B; C   D. A; B

38. According to the information in the above paragraph, a water extinguisher would MOST likely be suitable for use on which one of the following fires?
A(n)

    A. fire in a truck engine
    B. fire in an electrical switch
    C. oil fire
    D. lumber fire

39. According to the information in the above paragraph, dry chemical

    A. should not be used on a burning liquid fire
    B. is a conducting extinguishing agent
    C. should not be used on a fire in a car
    D. smothers fires to put them out

Questions 40-45.

DIRECTIONS: The table below shows the initial requests made by staff for vacation. It is to be used with the Rules and Guidelines to make the decisions and judgments called for in each of Questions 40 through 45.

VACATION REQUESTS FOR THE ONE YEAR PERIOD FROM MAY 1, YEAR X, THROUGH APRIL 30, YEAR Y

NAME	WORK ASSIGNMENT	DATE APPOINTED	ACCUMULATED ANNUAL LEAVE DAYS	VACATION PERIODS REQUESTED
DeMarco	MVO	Mar. 2003	25	May 3-21; Oct. 25-Nov. 5
Moore	Dispatcher	Dec. 1997	32	May 24-June 4; July 12-16
Kingston	MVO	Apr. 2007	28	May 24-June 11; Feb. 7-25
Green	MVO	June 2006	26	June 7-18; Sept. 6-24
Robinson	MVO	July 1998	30	June 28-July 9; Nov. 15-26
Reilly	MVO	Oct. 2009	23	July 5-9; Jan. 31-Mar. 3
Stevens	MVO	Sept. 1996	31	July 5-23; Oct. 4-29
Costello	MVO	Sept. 1998	31	July 5-30; Oct. 4-22
Maloney	Dispatcher	Aug. 1992	35	July 5-Aug. 6; Nov. 1-5
Hughes	Director	Feb. 1990	38	July 26-Sept. 3
Lord	MVO	Jan. 2010	20	Aug. 9-27; Feb. 7-25
Diaz	MVO	Dec. 2009	28	Aug. 9-Sept. 10
Krimsky	MVO	May 2006	22	Oct. 18-22; Nov. 22-Dec. 10

RULES AND GUIDELINES

1. The two dispatchers cannot be on vacation at the same time, nor can a dispatcher be on vacation at the same time as the director.

2. For the period June 1 through September 30, not more than three MVO's can be on vacation at the same time.

3. For the period October 1 through May 31, not more than two MVO's at a time can be on vacation.

4. In cases where the same vacation time is requested by too many employees for all of them to be given the time under the rules, the requests of those who have worked the longest will be granted.

5. No employee may take more leave days than the number of annual leave days accumulated and shown in the table.

6. All vacation periods shown in the table and described in the questions below begin on a Monday and end on a Friday.

7. Employees work a five day week (Monday through Friday). They are off weekends and holidays with no charges to leave balances. When a holiday falls on a Saturday or Sunday, employees are given the following Monday off without charge to annual leave.

8.   Holidays: May 31   October 25   January 1
                            July 4   November 2   February 12
                            September 6   November 25   February 21
                            October 11   December 25

9. An employee shall be given any part of his initial requests that is permissible under the above rules and shall have first right to it despite any further adjustment of schedule.

40. Until adjustments in the vacation schedule can be made, the vacation dates that can be approved for Krimsky are

    A.   Oct. 18-22; Nov. 22-Dec. 10
    B.   Oct. 18-22; Nov. 29-Dec. 10
    C.   Oct. 18-22 only
    D.   Nov. 22-Dec. 10 only

41. Until adjustments in the vacation schedule can be made, the vacation dates that can be approved for Maloney are

    A.   July 5-Aug. 6; Nov. 1-5
    B.   July 5-23; Nov. 1-5
    C.   July 5-9; Nov. 1-5
    D.   Nov. 1-5 only

42. According to the table, Lord wants a vacation in August and another in February. Until adjustments in the vacation schedule can be made, he can be allowed to take _____ of the August vacation _____ of the February vacation.

    A.   all; but none
    B.   all; and almost half
    C.   almost all; and almost half
    D.   almost half; and all

43. Costello cannot be given all the vacation he has requested because

    A.   the MVO's who have more seniority than he has have requested time he wishes
    B.   he does not have enough accumulated annual leave
    C.   a dispatcher is applying for vacation at the same time as Costello
    D.   there are five people who want vacation in July

44. According to the table, how many leave days will DeMarco be charged for his vacation from October 25 through November 5?

    A.   10   B.   9   C.   8   D.   7

45. How many leave days will Moore use if he uses the requested vacation allowable to him under the rules?

    A.   9   B.   10   C.   14   D.   15

KEY (CORRECT ANSWERS)

1. B	11. A	21. A	31. C	41. B
2. C	12. C	22. C	32. B	42. A
3. D	13. B	23. C	33. A	43. B
4. B	14. D	24. C	34. C	44. C
5. A	15. B	25. B	35. C	45. A
6. A	16. A	26. B	36. C	
7. C	17. D	27. B	37. B	
8. D	18. A	28. C	38. D	
9. D	19. A	29. B	39. D	
10. A	20. B	30. A	40. D	

EXAMINATION SECTION
TEST 1

DIRECTIONS: Each question or incomplete statement is followed by several suggested answers or completions. Select the one that BEST answers the question or completes the statement. *PRINT THE LETTER OF THE CORRECT ANSWER IN THE SPACE AT THE RIGHT.*

Questions 1-8.

DIRECTIONS: Questions 1 through 8, inclusive, are based on the paragraph *JACKS* shown below. When answering these questions, refer to this paragraph.

JACKS

When using a jack, a workman should cheek the capacity plate or other markings on the jack to make sure the device is heavy enough to support the load. Where there is no plate, capacity should be determined and painted on the side of the jack. The workman should see that jacks are well lubricated, but only at points where lubrication is specified, and should inspect them for broken teeth or faulty holding fixtures. A jack should never be thrown or dropped upon the floors such treatment may crack or distort the metal, thus causing the jack to break when a load is lifted. It is important that the floor or ground surface upon which the jack is placed be level and clean, and the safe limit of floor loading is not exceeded. If the surface is earth, the jack base should be set on heavy wood blocking, preferably hardwood, of sufficient size that the blocking will not turn over, shift, or sink. If the surface is not perfectly level, the jack may be set on blocking, which should be leveled by wedges securely placed so that they cannot be brushed or forced out of place. "Extenders" of wood or metal, intended to provide a higher rise where a jack cannot reach up to load or lift it high enough, should never be used. Instead, a larger jack should be obtained or higher blocking which is correspondingly wider and longer — should be placed under the jack. All lifts should be vertical with the jack correctly centered for the lift. The base of the jack should be on a perfectly level surface, and the jack head, with its hardwood shim, should bear against a perfectly level meeting surface.

1. To make sure the jack is heavy enough to support a certain load, the workman should   1.____

    A. lubricate the jack
    B. shim the jack
    C. check the capacity plate
    D. use a long handle

2. A jack should be lubricated   2.____

    A. after using
    B. before painting
    C. only at specified points
    D. to prevent slipping

3. The workman should inspect a jack for   3.____

    A. manufacturer's name
    B. broken teeth
    C. paint peeling
    D. broken wedges

4. Metal parts on a jack may crack if 4.____

   A. the jack is thrown on the floor
   B. the load is leveled
   C. blocking is used
   D. the handle is too short

5. It would NOT be a safe practice for a workman to 5.____

   A. center the jack under the load
   B. set the jack on a level surface
   C. use hardwood for blocking
   D. use *extenders* to reach up to the load

6. Wedges may safely be used to 6.____

   A. replace a broken tooth
   B. prevent the overloading of a jack
   C. level the blocking under a jack
   D. straighten distorted metal

7. Blocking should be 7.____

   A. made of a soft wood
   B. placed between the jack base and the earth surface
   C. well lubricated
   D. used to repair a broken tooth

8. A hardwood shim should be used 8.____

   A. between the head and its meeting surface
   B. under the jack
   C. as a filler
   D. to level a surface

9. When a long pipe is being carried, the front end should be held high and the rear end low. 9.____
   The MAIN reason for this is to

   A. prevent injury to others when turning blind corners
   B. make it easier to carry
   C. prevent injury to the man carrying the pipe
   D. prevent damage to the pipe

10. As a serviceman, you notice a condition in the shop which you believe to be dangerous, but is under the jurisdiction of another department. 10.____
    You should

    A. immediately notify your superior
    B. call the assistant general superintendent
    C. take no action, as your department is not involved
    D. send a letter to the department involved

11. All employees should regularly read the bulletin board at their job location MAINLY in order to

   A. learn what previously posted material has been removed
   B. show that they have an interest in the department
   C. see whether other employees have something for sale
   D. become familiar with new orders or procedures posted on it

12. The book of rules and regulations states that employees must give notice, in person or by telephone, at least one hour before they are scheduled to report for duty, of their intention to be absent from work.
   The LOGICAL reason for having this rule is that

   A. the employees' time can be recorded in advance
   B. a substitute can be provided
   C. it allows time to check the employees' record
   D. it reduces absenteeism

13. When tools are found in poor condition, the reason is MOST often because of

   A. misuse of tools
   B. their use by more than one person
   C. defects in the manufacture of tools
   D. their use in construction work

14. When lifting a heavy object, a man should NOT

   A. twist his body while lifting
   B. bend knees
   C. have secure footing
   D. take a firm grip on the object

15. The MAIN purpose of the periodic inspection of machines and equipment is to

   A. locate stolen property
   B. make the workmen more familiar with the equipment
   C. discover minor faults before they develop into more serious conditions
   D. encourage the workmen to take better care of their equipment

16. If a serviceman does not understand a verbal order given him by his foreman, he should

   A. do the best he can
   B. ask for a different assignment
   C. ask the foreman to explain it
   D. look it up in the book of rules

17. A rule prohibits indulgence in intoxicating liquor, or being under its influence, while on duty. This rule is rigidly enforced in order to

   A. prevent an employee from endangering himself or others
   B. help reduce littering
   C. eliminate absenteeism
   D. help promote temperance

18. As a newly appointed serviceman, your foreman would expect you to

   A. make many blunders
   B. repair car equipment
   C. study car maintenance on your own time
   D. follow his instructions closely

19. Your work will probably be MOST appreciated by your superior if you

   A. continually ask questions about your work
   B. keep him informed whenever you think someone has violated a rule
   C. continually come to him with suggestions for improving the job
   D. do your share by completing assigned tasks properly and on time

20. One of your fellow workers has to leave work a half-hour early and asks you to punch his time card for him.
    You should

   A. punch out for him, but be sure to tell your supervisor
   B. tell him that no one is allowed to punch out someone else's time card
   C. punch out for him because you know he would do the same for you
   D. tell him he must promise to stay an extra half-hour tomorrow before you punch out for him

21. As far as is practicable, fiber rope should not be allowed to become wet, as this hastens decay. The MOST logical conclusion to be drawn from this statement is that

   A. fiber rope is stronger than nylon rope
   B. shrinkage of wet rope is not a problem
   C. nylon rope is better than wire rope
   D. wet rope should be thoroughly dried before being stored away

22. The MAIN reason that gear cases are stacked on a pallet is to

   A. help servicemen find gear cases quickly
   B. help stockmen keep track of gear cases
   C. avoid hand-carrying of gear cases
   D. prevent damage to gear cases

23. If you are holding a heavy load by the pull rope on a block and tackle, your BEST procedure is to

   A. let the rope hang loose
   B. snub the rope around a fixed object
   C. pull sideways to jam the rope in the block
   D. stand on the rope and hold the end

24. Modern electric power tools such as electric drills come with a third conductor in the power cord, which is used to connect the case of the tool to a grounded part of the electric outlet.
    The reason for this additional electrical conductor is to

A. protect the user of the tool should the motor short out to the case
B. provide for continued operation of the tool should the regular grounded line-wire open
C. eliminate sparking between the tool and the material being worked upon
D. provide a spare wire for additional controls

25. When a long ladder is being used, a length of rope should be tied from its lowest rung to a fixed support in order to prevent 25._____

   A. breaking the rungs
   B. the ladder from slipping
   C. anyone from removing the ladder
   D. anyone from walking under the ladder

26. When the level of the liquid in a storage battery on a Hi-lo truck is too low, the proper liquid to add to bring the level up to normal is 26._____

   A. salt   B. alkaline solution
   C. acid solution   D. distilled water

27. The MOST important reason for servicemen to keep their work areas neat and clean is that it 27._____

   A. makes more room for storage
   B. makes for happier workers
   C. prevents tools from being broken
   D. decreases the chances of accidents to workmen

28. The one of the following which is the BEST example of a material that does NOT burn easily is 28._____

   A. canvas   B. paper   C. wood   D. asbestos

29. The CHIEF reason for not letting oily rags or dust cloths accumulate in storage closets is that they 29._____

   A. look dirty
   B. may start a fire by spontaneous combustion
   C. take up space which may be used for more important purposes
   D. may drip oil onto the floor

30. The MOST logical reason for a serviceman to blow out electrical and mechanical equipment under car bodies before they are worked on by maintainers is to 30._____

   A. cool the equipment for the maintainers
   B. prevent rusting of equipment and parts
   C. prevent the maintainers from getting dirty while working
   D. prevent fires caused by heavy accumulation of dust

31. The liquid in heavy duty hydraulic jacks used in the car shops is 31._____

   A. water   B. oil   C. mercury   D. alcohol

32. It is not considered good practice to paint portable wooden ladders. 32.____
    The MOST logical reason for this is that the paint

    A. would quickly wear off
    B. might hide serious defects
    C. might rub off on a supporting wall
    D. would dry out the rungs

33. In order to lift a loaded pallet overhead by means of a crane, it would be MOST desirable 33.____
    to use a

    A. single wire rope sling   B. long crowbar
    C. pallet sling   D. rope splice

34. Of the following methods, the one which is the BEST way to keep rust off metal tools is to 34.____

    A. keep them dry and oil them once in a while
    B. air blast them
    C. file or grind them often
    D. wash them carefully with warm water

35. A Hi-Lo truck delivering a compressor to a work area approaches a closed door. 35.____
    The proper procedure for the Hi-Lo operator to follow is to

    A. open the door while standing on the operating end of the Hi-Lo truck
    B. open the door with the platform of the Hi-Lo truck
    C. stop the Hi-Lo truck, wedge open the door, and then proceed
    D. make a detour and follow a different path

36. The path between the two yellow lines on a main shop floor is used for 36.____

    A. picking up and discharging workers that want a ride on a Hi-Lo
    B. parking area for forklifts
    C. the traffic path for Hi-Lo's and forklifts
    D. storage of materials unloaded from Hi-Lo's

37. While on the way to a storeroom, you notice that oil has dripped on the floor from a jour- 37.____
    nal box and created a slipping hazard.
    You should

    A. ignore it as it is not your doing
    B. get some *speedi-dry* nearby and spread it over the oil
    C. wait until you return from the storeroom to take care of it
    D. call the supervisor and tell him about it

38. An employee always obeys the safety rules of his department because it has become a 38.____
    habit to work by these rules. This is

    A. *good;* such a habit will get work done safely
    B. *bad;* it is hard to change a habit
    C. *good;* safety rules won't work if they have to be thought about
    D. *bad;* safety rules should always be thought about before doing anything and not
       allowed to become a habit

39. If *you* are working in an inspection shop and you notice a trolley bug on one contact shoe of a car, it will mean that

    A. all contact shoes of the car are *live*
    B. only that contact shoe, that the bug is on, is *live*
    C. only the contact shoes, on the same side of the car that the bug is on, are *live*
    D. only the contact shoes of the one truck are *live*

39.____

40. It is necessary for a serviceman to wear a respirator when he is

    A. climbing a ladder
    B. operating a chipping gun
    C. blowing out the equipment under a car
    D. lubricating gear cases

40.____

KEY (CORRECT ANSWERS)

1. C	11. D	21. D	31. B
2. C	12. B	22. C	32. B
3. B	13. A	23. B	33. C
4. A	14. A	24. A	34. A
5. D	15. C	25. B	35. C
6. C	16. C	26. D	36. C
7. B	17. A	27. D	37. B
8. A	18. D	28. D	38. A
9. A	19. D	29. B	39. A
10. A	20. B	30. D	40. C

TEST 2

DIRECTIONS: Each question or incomplete statement is followed by several suggested answers or completions. Select the one that BEST answers the question or completes the statement. *PRINT THE LETTER OF THE CORRECT ANSWER IN THE SPACE AT THE RIGHT.*

1. The type of fire extinguisher which you would NOT use to extinguish a fire around electrical circuits is 1.____

    A. carbon dioxide
    B. dry chemical
    C. water
    D. dry sand

2. Artificial respiration is applied when an accident has caused 2.____

    A. breathing difficulties
    B. loss of blood
    C. broken ribs
    D. burns

3. Workers must NOT wear clothes that are too big when they work near moving machinery because 3.____

    A. that kind of dress will attract attention
    B. some part of the clothes can catch in the machinery
    C. big clothes get dirtier
    D. big clothes are hard to replace

4. The MOST likely reason why an employee should make out a report after using the contents of a first aid kit is that 4.____

    A. he will learn to write a good report
    B. unauthorized use may be prevented
    C. used material will be replaced
    D. a new seal may be provided

5. A shop employee is involved in an accident and severely injures his ankle. If a tourniquet were used, it would be to 5.____

    A. keep the ankle warm
    B. prevent infection
    C. prevent the ankle from moving
    D. stop the loss of blood

6. If a serviceman has frequent accidents, it is MOST likely that he is 6.____

    A. a man who works best by himself
    B. satisfied with his job
    C. violating too many safety rules
    D. simply one of those persons who is unlucky

7. In treating a cut finger, the FIRST action should be to 7.____

    A. wash it
    B. bandage it
    C. request sick leave
    D. apply antiseptic

8. When administering first aid to a person suffering from shock as a result of an accident, it is MOST important to 8.____

54

A. keep him moving
B. prop him up in a sitting position
C. apply artificial respiration
D. cover the person and keep him warm

9. First aid instructions are given to some employees to   9._____

   A. eliminate the need for calling a doctor
   B. prepare them to give emergency aid
   C. collect blood for the blood bank
   D. reduce the number of accidents

10. The BEST reason for not using compressed air from an air hose for cleaning dust from   10._____
    clothing is that

    A. the clothing may be torn by the blast
    B. it is a dangerous practice
    C. this air contains too much moisture
    D. the air pressure will drop too low

11. Protective helmets give servicemen the MOST protection from   11._____

    A. falling objects   B. fire
    C. eye injuries   D. electric shock

12. Fuses are used in electric circuits   12._____

    A. so that electrical power tools cannot short circuit
    B. to burn out under an overload before electrical equipment is damaged
    C. to increase the amount of current that may be carried in the wires
    D. so that workmen can cut off the current without looking for the switch

13. The one of the following that is MOST effective in reducing the danger from hazardous   13._____
    vapors is

    A. immediate disposal of all wastes
    B. labeling all substances clearly
    C. maintaining good ventilation
    D. wearing proper clothing at all times

14. A serviceman should NEVER look into the arc from an electric welding torch.   14._____
    The BEST reason for this is that

    A. it can have a harmful effect on his eyes
    B. it will distract the welder from his work
    C. the serviceman is not allowed to operate a welding torch
    D. electric arc welding uses a large electrical current

15. The floors of 2 cars are to be painted with a special test paint. Assume that the floor area   15._____
    in each car is 600 square feet. A gallon of this paint will cover 400 square feet.
    The number of gallons of this paint that you should pick up at the storeroom to paint
    the 2 car floors would be

    A. 6   B. 5   C. 4   D. 3

16. Assume that you are sent to the storeroom for 1,000 of 600-volt contact tips which are to be distributed equally to 5 foremen, but you find that the storeroom can only supply you with 825.
   If you distribute these 825 tips equally to the 5 foremen, the number of tips that each foreman will receive is

   A. 165   B. 175   C. 190   D. 200

17. You are asked to fill six 5-gallon cans of oil from a full drum containing 52 gallons. When you have filled the six cans, the number of gallons of oil left in the drun will be MOST NEARLY

   A. 14   B. 16   C. 22   D. 30

18. A certain wire rope is made up of 6 strands, each strand containing 19 wires.
   The total number of wires in this wire rope is

   A. 25   B. 96   C. 114   D. 144

19. The hook should be the weakest part of any crane, hoist, or sling.
   According to this statement, if a particular hook has a rated capacity of 21/2 tons, then the MAXIMUM load thatshould be lifted with this hook is _____ pounds.

   A. 150   B. 3,000   C. 5,000   D. 5,500

20. Assume that 2 car wheels weigh 635 pounds each and are attached to an axle weighing 1,260 pounds.
   The total weight of this assembly is MOST NEARLY _____ pounds.

   A. 1,270   B. 1,520   C. 1,895   D. 2,530

21. If an employee authorizes his employer to deduct 4% of his $450 weekly salary for a savings bond, the MINIMUM number of weekly deductions required to get enough money to buy a bond costing $54 is

   A. 3   B. 6   C. 8   D. 9

22. In weighing out a truckful of scrap metal, the scale reads 21,496 lbs. If the empty truck weighs 9,879 lbs., the amount of scrap metal, in pounds, is MOST NEARLY

   A. 10,507   B. 10,602   C. 11,617   D. 12,617

23. Four trays of material are placed on the body of a delivery truck for delivery to the inspection shop. Each tray is 4 feet wide and 4 feet long.
   If these trays are placed side by side on the floor of the delivery truck, together they will cover an area of the floor MOST NEARLY _____ square feet.

   A. 32   B. 48   C. 64   D. 72

24. Assume that you are operating a degreasing tank and its tray holds 5 gear cases. It takes 40 minutes to clean one tray of gear cases.
   At the end of 6 hours of operation (excluding lunch break and loading and unloading time), the number of gear cases cleaned will be

   A. 30   B. 36   C. 45   D. 50

25. If a serviceman's weekly gross salary is $480, and 20% is deducted for taxes, his take-home pay is

   A. $360　　B. $384　　C. $420　　D. $432

26. Two-thirds of 10 feet is MOST NEARLY

   A. 6'2"　　B. 6'8"　　C. 6'11"　　D. 7'1"

27. You are directed to pick up a tray load of brake shoes.
   The combined weight of tray and brake shoes is 4,000 pounds. Assume that each brake shoe weighs 40 pounds and the tray weighs 240 pounds.
   The number of brake shoes in the tray is MOST NEARLY

   A. 88　　B. 94　　C. 100　　D. 106

28. The one of the following materials that is used to protect equipment from rain is a

   A. sprinkler　　　B. tarpaulin
   C. compressor　　D. templet

29. The use of wet rope near power lines and other electrical equipment is

   A. a dangerous practice
   B. sure to interrupt telephone service
   C. recommended as a safe practice
   D. common in the car shop but not in maintenance of way

Questions 30-34.

DIRECTIONS: Questions 30 through 34, inclusive, are based on the following paragraph, table, and floor plan. Each line in the table contains the name of a certain piece of car equipment together with its destination in the car shop. The floor plan shows a car shop divided into six areas, each with a different code number.

TABLE

NAME OF CAR EQUIPMENT	DESTINATION IN CAR SHOP
Journal boxes	Degreasing tanks
Door operators	Car body shop Main
Air compressors	shipping Air brake shop
Unit valves	Truck shop Degreasing
Wheels Gear assemblies	tanks Main shipping
Unit switches Variable load units	Air brake shop
Motor couplings	Degreasing tanks
Motors Brake linkage	Truck shop Degreasing
Fan motors Batteries	tanks Car body shop
Motor generators	Main shipping Car body shop

CAR SHOP FLOOR PLAN

Overhaul Shop	Air Brake Shop	Main Shipping
AREA 1	AREA 2	AREA 3
Degreasing Tanks	Truck Shop	
AREA 4	AREA 5	
Car Body Shop AREA 6		

In each of Questions 30 through 34, there are the names of four types of car equipment, and a code number for a destination in the car shop. In each question, select the CORRECT combination of equipment name and destination code number as determined by referring to the Table and Car Shop Floor Plan.

30.
- A. Motor generators: Area 6
- B. Fan motors: Area 5
- C. Motor couplings: Area 1
- D. Motor end housings: Area 2

30._____

31.
- A. Door operators: Area 3
- B. Air compressors: Area 5
- C. Brake linkage: Area 4
- D. Variable load units: Area 6

31._____

32.
- A. Batteries: Area 1
- B. Unit switches: Area 3
- C. Motor controllers: Area 2
- D. Fan motors: Area 4

32._____

33.
- A. Wheels: Area 2
- B. Motor end housings: Area 6
- C. Journal boxes: Area 3
- D. Unit valves: Area 2

33._____

34.
- A. Gear assemblies: Area 4
- B. Motor couplings: Area 3
- C. Variable load units: Area 6
- D. Unit valves: Area 5

34._____

35. The drawing at the right is an assembly sketch. Study the sketch and select the CORRECT assembly procedure.
- A. 3 onto 4, 2 onto 5, 1 onto 5, and tighten
- B. 4 onto 3, 1 onto 5, 5 through 4 and 3, tighten 2 onto 5
- C. 5 into 3, 2 and 1 onto 5, 4 into 3, and tighten
- D. 4 into 3, 5 through 3 and 4, 2 onto 5, 1 onto 5, and tighten

35._____

Questions 36-37.

DIRECTIONS: Questions 36 and 37 are based on the following data and sketch. When answering these questions, refer to this material.

The average clearance requirements for 2-ton, 3-ton, and 5-ton forklift trucks are shown in the following sketch. Dimensions are: R, the overall length including loads S, the overall widths T, the overall height; U, the minimum permissible width of aisle.

	2-Ton Truck	3-Ton Truck	5-Ton Truck
B	112	118	142
S	45	46	47
T	85	85	85
U	76	79	92

All dimensions are in inches.

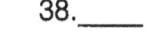

36. From the data given above, it can be seen that the overall length, including load, of a 3-ton truck is _____ inches.

    A. 85   B. 92   C. 118   D. 142

37. From the data given above, it can be seen that the overall height of a 2-ton truck is _____ inches.

    A. 47   B. 76   C. 79   D. 85

38.

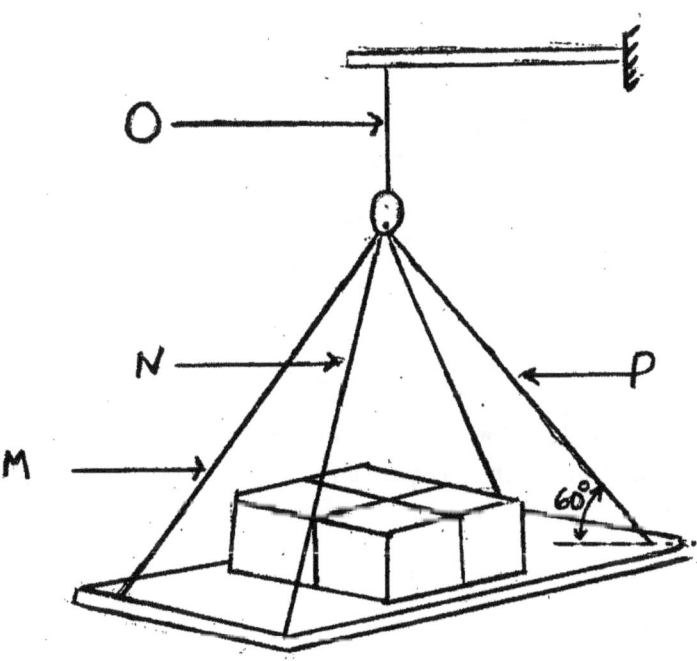

The above diagram shows a loaded sling suspended from a crane. The rope which carries the heaviest load is

    A. M   B. N   C. O   D. P

39. If the tray shown in the diagram at the right is being pushed in the direction shown by the arrows, it is MOST likely to move in the direction of the arrow shown in

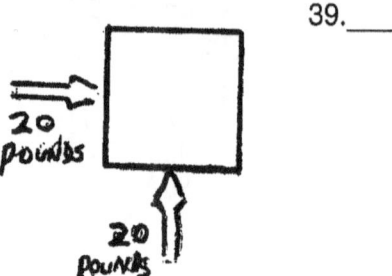

A.

B.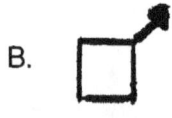

C.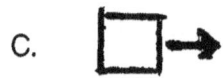

D.

40.

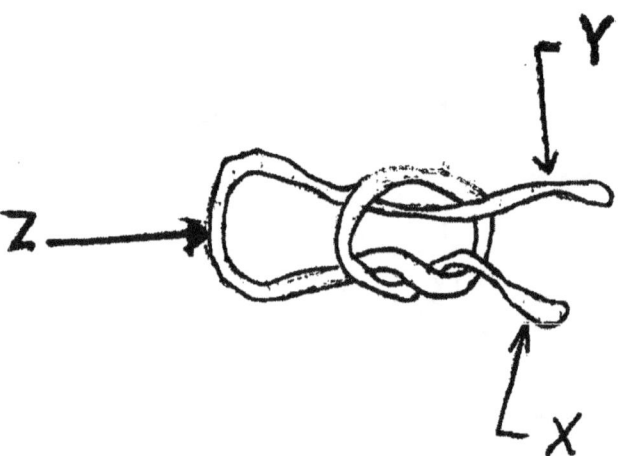

The above diagram shows a slip knot. The way this knot is nade, it would be CORRECT to say that the knot can be untied by pulling on line _____ while holding _____.

A. X; line Z
B. Y; line X
C. X and line Y together; line Z
D. Z; lines X and Y together

KEY (CORRECT ANSWERS)

1. C	11. A	21. A	31. C
2. A	12. B	22. C	32. B
3. B	13. C	23. C	33. D
4. C	14. A	24. C	34. A
5. D	15. D	25. B	35. D
6. C	16. A	26. B	36. C
7. A	17. C	27. B	37. D
8. D	18. C	28. B	38. C
9. B	19. C	29. A	39. B
10. B	20. D	30. A	40. B

EXAMINATION SECTION
TEST 1

DIRECTIONS: Each question or incomplete statement is followed by several suggested answers or completions. Select the one that BEST answers the question or completes the statement. *PRINT THE LETTER OF THE CORRECT ANSWER IN THE SPACE AT THE RIGHT.*

1. Front stabilizer bars on automotive vehicles are set in such a manner that they 1.____
    A. apply force opposite to that of the springs when the springs are deflected equally
    B. normally connect to both lower control arms
    C. are adjustable in order to level the vehicle
    D. have one end attached to the lower control arm and the other end attached to the frame

2. Ignition point contact alignment is BEST adjusted by bending the 2.____
    A. movable point arm   B. pivot post
    C. breaker plate   D. stationary point bracket

3. When disc brakes are retracted so as not to be touching the braking disc, the amount of retraction 3.____
    A. is affected by the piston return springs
    B. must be a minimum of 1/32 of an inch
    C. is affected by the piston seals
    D. is limited by the metering valve

4. A PROPERLY operating positive crankcase ventilation valve will 4.____
    A. control air flow as a direct function of engine speed
    B. increase air flow in direct proportion to the increase in manifold vacuum
    C. shut off air flow at high intake manifold vacuum
    D. reduce air flow at high intake manifold vacuum

5. The air-fuel ratio, by weight, in a properly functioning gasoline automotive engine is MOST NEARLY 5.____
    A. 15:1   B. 30:1   C. 600:1   D. 9000:1

6. Cam ground pistons are distinguished by 6.____
    A. being ground perfectly round
    B. having a larger diameter across the piston pin faces
    C. having a larger diameter parallel to the crankshaft centerline
    D. having a larger diameter perpendicular to the crankshaft centerline

7. In an automotive engine, the intake valves USUALLY open _____ TDC and close _____ BDC of the intake stroke. 7.____
    A. after; after   B. after; before
    C. before; before   D. before; after

8. In an automotive engine, the exhaust valves USUALLY open _____ BDC of the power stroke and _____ TDC of the intake stroke.
   A. after; before
   B. before; before
   C. before; after
   D. after; after

9. The PRIMARY function of a blower on a two-cycle diesel engine is to
   A. provide air for scavenging
   B. increase the compression ratio
   C. blow in the fuel-air mixture
   D. cool the oil after compression in the injector pump

10. Excessive free travel of the clutch pedal would be indicated if the
    A. transmission was hard to shift smoothly
    B. clutch slipped when fully engaged
    C. throwout bearing failed prematurely
    D. release levers were worn

11. Vacuum is usually referred to in inches of mercury.
    The number of pounds per square inch pressure above zero (absolute pressure) of a 20 inch vacuum is MOST NEARLY
    A. 4.9
    B. 7.4
    C. 9.6
    D. 11.8

12. Only a portion of the heat energy released by the gasoline in an automotive engine is transmitted to the wheels for driving purposes.
    In an automobile in good condition and with an efficiently operating engine, this portion is MOST NEARLY
    A. 90%
    B. 50%
    C. 20%
    D. 2%

13. An adjustment is made to the right front wheel of a vehicle equipped with shims at the junction of the upper suspension arm and the frame support by moving the upper suspension arm away from the frame a greater amount in the front than in the rear. This is done to
    A. increase the steering knuckle angle
    B. adjust the caster in a negative direction
    C. adjust the camber in a negative direction
    D. adjust the caster in a rotary direction

14. In an automotive rear axle in which the pinion gear engages the ring gear below the centerline of the axle, the cut of the pinion and ring gear is
    A. spiral bevel
    B. spur bevel
    C. double helical
    D. hypoid

15. Of the following statements concerning the operation in low gear of a fully synchronized (in forward gears) three-speed transmission, the one that is NOT correct is that
    A. both clutch sleeves must engage gears
    B. power is being transmitted through the countershaft gears
    C. one clutch sleeve must be engaged
    D. the reverse idler gear is being driven by a countershaft gear

Questions 16-17.

DIRECTIONS: Questions 16 and 17 are to be answered in accordance with the following paragraph.

Steam cleaners get their name from the fact that steam is used to generate pressure and is also a by-product of heating the cleaning solution. Steam itself as little cleaning power. It will melt some soils, but it does not dissolve them, break them up, or destroy their clinging power. Rather surprisingly, good machines generate as little steam as possible. Modern surface chemistry depends on a chemical solution to dissolve dirt, destroy its clinging power, and hold it in suspension. Steam actually hinders such a solution, but heat helps its physical and chemical action. Cleaning is most efficient when a hot solution reaches the work in heavy volume.

16. In accordance with the above paragraph, for MOST efficient cleaning,
    A. a heavy volume of steam is needed
    B. hot steam is needed to break up the soils
    C. steam is used to dissolve the surface dirt
    D. a hot chemical solution should always be used

    16._____

17. When reference to the above paragraph, the steam in a steam cleaner is used to
    A. generate pressure
    B. create by-product chemicals
    C. slow down the chemical action of the cleaning solution
    D. dissolve accumulations of dirt

    17._____

18. An electromechanical regulator for an automotive alternator differs from a DC generator in that the alternator regulator
    A. has a current regulator unit
    B. has a reverse current relay
    C. does not have a current regulator unit
    D. does not have a voltage regulator unit

    18._____

19. Of the following statements concerning the charging of lead acid batteries, the one MOST NEARLY correct is that
    A. a fast charge (40-50 amp, 2V) can safely be used if the battery temperature does not exceed 185° F
    B. heavily sulphated batteries respond best to a slow charging rate
    C. a battery on trickle charge cannot be damaged by overcharging
    D. the higher the battery temperature, the smaller the charging current with constant applied voltage

    19._____

20. The ignition points of a conventional ignition system are adjusted to increase the point gap.
    This adjustment will
    A. increase the dwell angle
    B. retard the ignition timing
    C. advance the ignition timing
    D. decrease the dwell angle with no change in ignition timing

    20._____

4 (#1)

21. A single diaphragm distributor vacuum advance unit   21.____
    A. advances the spark under part throttle operation
    B. is connected to the intake manifold
    C. advances the spark in proportion to engine speed
    D. advances the spark during acceleration or full throttle operation

22. The part of a conventional ignition system that could properly be considered   22.____
    part of BOTH the primary and secondary circuits would be the
    A. condenser   B. distributor rotor
    C. coil   D. ignition points

23. As compared to a conventional type of spark plug, a resistor type of spark   23.____
    plug will
    A. reduce the inductive portion of the spark
    B. lengthen the capacitive portion of the spark
    C. require a higher voltage to function properly
    D. have an auxiliary air gap

24. If the criterion that limits the yearly major repair expenses to 30% of the current   24.____
    value of equipment were reduced to 15% and the depreciation rate of 20% of
    original cost each year were increased to 25%, the expenses for major repairs
    in a shop handling a constant flow of equipment of the same type and age
    would
    A. increase slightly   B. remain the same
    C. increase slightly   D. increase markedly

Question 25.

DIRECTIONS: Question 25 is to be answered in accordance with the following paragraph.

   The storage battery is a lead-acid, electrochemical device used for storing energy in its
chemical form. The battery does not actually store electricity, but converts an electrical charge
into chemical energy which is stored until the battery terminals are connected to a closed
external circuit. When the circuit is closed, the chemical energy inside the battery is
transformed back into electrical energy through a chemical action, and, as a result, current flows
through the circuit.

25. According to the above paragraph, a lead-acid battery stores   25.____
    A. current   B. electricity
    C. electrical energy   D. chemical energy

26. A cam is to be fashioned from a circular disc with a hole drilled eccentrically   26.____
    on a diameter of the disc but perpendicularly to the surface of the disc. A
    keyed shaft is to be fitted into the hole so that the disc may be rotated in order
    to function as a cam. If the disc is 5 inches in diameter and ½ inch thick and
    the hole is to be 1 inch in diameter, the distance from the center of the disc to
    the center of the hole to be drilled in order for the disc to act as a cam with a 2
    inch lift should be _____ inch(es).
    A. 2   B. 1½   C. 1   D. ½

27. Sparks and open flames should be kept away from batteries that are being charged because of the danger of explosion or fire resulting from the ignition of the generated _____ gas.
   A. fluorine   B. nitrogen   C. hydrogen   D. argon

28. Safety standards indicate that the use of any motor vehicle equipment having an obstructed view to the rear
   A. requires a reverse signal alarm audible above the surrounding noise level
   B. requires the use of two back-up lights of at least 45 watt capacity each
   C. requires the use of a safety contact alarm rear bumper audible above the surrounding noise level
   D. is prohibited

29. In the performance of a compression test, it is found that the addition of a tablespoon of SAE 40 motor oil causes no significant increase in the low compression pressure.
   The low compression pressure is most probably NOT caused by
   A. a broken piston   B. a leaking head gasket
   C. sticking valves   D. worn piston rings

30. Automotive exhaust gas analyzers, as generally used in emission control maintenance, will normally indicate the percentage of
   A. NO   B. SO_2 C. CO_2 D. CO

Questions 31-33.

DIRECTIONS: Questions 31 through 33 are to be answered in accordance with the information given below.

For most efficient utilization of funds and facilities, the rule has been established that the repair cost of a part cannot exceed 50% of the vendor's price for a new part and that a part cannot be made in-house if the cost would be more than 70% of the vendor's price for a new one.

You have found that the average removed sprocket shaft, as shown below, requires both bearing sections to be built up and remachined and one sprocket section to be built up and remachined. The foreman of the machine shop has given you the following information relative to the manufacture or repair of the shafts:

	Time	Rate
Weld 1 bearing section	1.2 hours	$40/hr.
Weld 1 keyway and sprocket section	2.0 hours	$40/hr.
Turn 1 bearing section	0.6 hours	$40/hr.
Turn 1 sprocket section	0.7 hours	$40/hr.
Cut 1 keyway	0.5 hours	$40/hr.

Purchasing has quoted shaft material at $60/ft. and new shafts at $800 each.

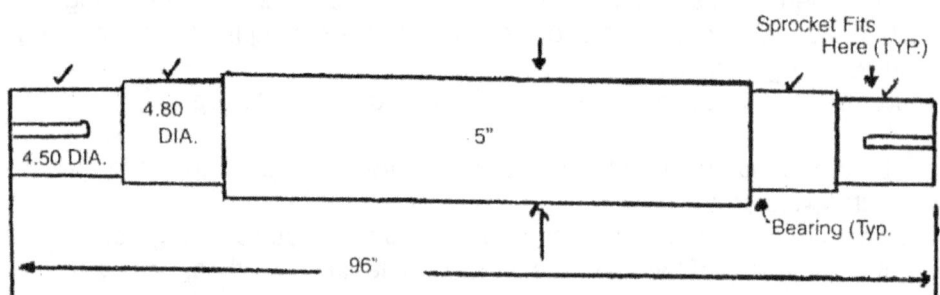

31. In accordance with the information given above, the cost for in-house manufacture of one shaft is
    A. $552.00   B. $560.00   C. $624.00   D. $663.00

32. In accordance with the information given above, the cost of in-house repair of one shaft is
    A. $342.00   B. $272.00   C. $152.00   D. $72.00

33. In accordance with the information given above, the PROPER procedure to follow, under the given rules, is to
    A. repair old shafts and buy new shafts
    B. repair old shafts and make new shafts
    C. make no repairs but make new shafts
    D. make no repairs but buy new shafts

34. The series of small vertical oscillations in the area of the center of a superimposed pattern on the screen of a properly adjusted oscilloscope showing the secondary circuit of a properly tuned automotive engine directly follows the instant at which the
    A. spark plugs fire   B. points open
    C. points close   D. coil starts to discharge

35. A rectangularly shaped repair facility for light trucks is 160 feet wide and 260 feet long. A 10 foot space is provided along each wall for benches and equipment. A 60 foot wide area in the middle of the floor is to remain clear for its entire 260 foot length. The entrance to the shop is at one end of this open area.
    Assuming that there are no columns to contend with, the MAXIMUM area available for parking of trucks is _____ square feet.
    A. 15,600   B. 19,200   C. 26,000   D. 42,600

36. A criterion is established that limits the early major repair expenses to 30% of the current value of the equipment. Equipment is depreciated at a rate of 20% of its original cost each year. A truck purchased on January 1, 2020 for $9,000 had a reconditioned engine installed in February 2023 at a total cost of $900. The amount of money available for additional major repairs on this truck in 2023 was
    A. none   B. $180   C. $360   D. $720

37. Twenty fuel injectors are ordered for your shop by the purchasing department. The terms are list, less 30%, less 10%, less 5%.
If the list price of a fuel injector is $70 and all terms ae met upon delivery, the charges to your budget will be
   A. $1,359.60   B. $1,085.40   C. $837.90   D. $630.80

38. The cylinders of an 8 cylinder automotive engine have a bore of 4 inches and the pistons have a stroke of 4 inches.
If the clearance volume in each cylinder is 6.0 cubic inches, the cubic inch displacement of the engine is MOST NEARLY
   A. 306   B. 354   C. 402   D. 450

39. An automotive engine cylinder has a bore of 4 inches and its pistons have a stroke of 4 inches.
If the clearance volume in the cylinder is 6.0 cubic inches, the compression ratio is MOST NEARLY
   A. 10.62:1   B. 9.37:1   C. 8.37:1   D. 7.62:1

40. Of the following deficiencies found during the inspection of passenger car brakes for issuance of a State Certificate of Inspection, the one that would be cause for REJECTION of the car brakes is that
   A. there is less than 3/64 in. of lining remaining above the drum brake shoe lining rivet heads
   B. the master cylinder brake fluid level is anything less than full
   C. the brake drums have been found to be more than .020 inches oversize
   D. the brake pedal reserve is less than one-half the total possible travel

41. When checking a fuel pump for proper operation, it is ALWAYS necessary to
   A. connect a vacuum gage to the fuel line between the pump and the carburetor
   B. make the vacuum test before the pressure test
   C. set the gages at floor level to maintain a consistent reference point
   D. make a vacuum test if the pressure or volume test results are not up to specification

42. On a single cylinder 4 stroke cycle internal combustion engine equipped with a flywheel magneto, the ignition points open at the end of the _____ strokes.
   A. intake and the compression   B. compression and the exhaust
   C. power and the compression   D. intake and the power

43. An impulse coupling is MOST usually found in
   A. an automatic transmission
   B. a limited slip differential
   C. the front axle of 4 wheel drive vehicles
   D. a magneto

8 (#1)

Questions 44-45.

DIRECTIONS: Questions 44 and 45 are to be answered in accordance with the following paragraph.

You have been instructed to expedite the fabrication of four special salt spreader trucks using chassis that are available in the shop. All four trucks must be delivered before the opening of business on December 1, 2021. Based on workload and available hours, the foreman of the body shop indicates that he could manufacture one complete salt spreader body in five weeks, with one additional week required for mounting and securing each body to the available chassis. No work could begin on the body until the engines and hydraulic components, which would have to be purchased, were available for use. The purchasing department has promised delivery of engines and hydraulic components three months after the order is placed. (Assume that all months have four weeks and the same crew is doing the assembling and manufacturing.)

44. With reference to the above paragraph, assuming that the purchasing department placed the order at the beginning of the first week in February 2020 and ultimate delivery of the firs salt spreader truck would be CLOSEST to the end of the _____ week in _____, 2021.
    A. fourth; July
    B. second; August
    C. fourth; August
    D. first; September

44._____

45. With reference to the above paragraph, the LATEST date that the engines and associated hydraulic components could be requisitioned in order to meet the specified deadline would be CLOSEST to the beginning of the _____ week in _____, 2021.
    A. first; February
    B. first; March
    C. third; March
    D. first; April

45._____

46. In an OHV internal combustion engine, excessive inlet valve guide clearance manifests itself initially by
    A. lowered cylinder compression pressure
    B. excessive oil consumption
    C. increased manifold vacuum
    D. fluffy black deposits on spark plugs

46._____

47. One of your mechanics has performed an automotive fuel system test and reports a fuel flow of ½ pint/minute at 500 rpm, a static fuel pump discharge pressure of 6 psi, and a 15 in.Hg vacuum at the pump inlet flex line.
These results should suggest to the mechanic that
    A. the system was operating properly
    B. he should check for a leaking pump inlet flex line
    C. he should replace the defective fuel pump
    D. check for a plugged inlet fuel line

47._____

9 (#1)

48. An electrician is wiring a light switch on a light truck. The light switch will operate the following lamp bulbs:

Quantity	No.	Description	Current (Each)
2	194	Marker	.3
3	67	Clearance	.4
2	1157	Stop/Tail	2.1/.6
2	1141	Front Park	1.5
2	6012	Headlamp	4.2/3.4

The parking lamps are to be on when the headlamps are on.
If the permissible current capacities of wire are
    16 gage   0 – 6 amp
    14 gage   6 – 15 amp
    12 gage   15 – 20 amp
    10 gage   20 – 25 amp,
the smallest size wire that the electrician should use to supply power to the switch would be a _____ gage wire.
    A. 16   B. 14   C. 12   D. 10

49. In an automotive cooling system, the bypass passage or bypass valve
    A. permits a small amount of coolant to pass around the thermostat to maintain circulation
    B. permits the circulation of coolant through the engine block when the thermostat is closed
    C. directly connects the pump inlet to the pump discharge to prevent cavitation in the pump
    D. prevents the coolant in the system from developing excessive pressure

50. When adjusting a recirculating ball worm-and-nut steering gear, it is IMPROPER procedure to
    A. remove the pitman arm before making adjustments
    B. loosen the lash adjustment before checking bearing preload
    C. make the pitman shaft gear over center adjustment with the steering wheel in the center of travel position
    D. adjust the bearing preload with the steering wheel in the center of travel position

KEY (CORRECT ANSWERS)

1. B	11. A	21. A	31. C	41. D
2. D	12. C	22. C	32. B	42. B
3. C	13. B	23. A	33. A	43. D
4. D	14. D	24. A	34. C	44. A
5. A	15. A	25. D	35. B	45. B
6. D	16. D	26. C	36. B	46. B
7. D	17. A	27. C	37. C	47. D
8. C	18. C	28. A	38. C	48. B
9. A	19. B	29. D	39. B	49. B
10. A	20. C	30. D	40. B	50. D

EXAMINATION SECTION
TEST 1

DIRECTIONS: Each question or incomplete statement is followed by several suggested answers or completions. Select the one that BEST answers the question or completes the statement. *PRINT THE LETTER OF THE CORRECT ANSWER IN THE SPACE AT THE RIGHT.*

1. Piston rings are used to
   A. keep the piston from wearing
   B. prevent leakage of gas into the crankcase
   C. keep the cylinder walls smooth
   D. reduce the friction between the cylinder walls and the piston

   1.____

2. By camber is meant the
   A. forward tilt of the king pin
   B. backward tilt of the king pin
   C. outward tilt of the front wheels from the vertical
   D. difference of the distance between the front wheels at the front and at the rear of the front wheels

   2.____

3. An engine develops more torque when the car is
   A. rounding a curve
   B. going down a hill
   C. in low speed
   D. in high speed

   3.____

4. When the brakes of a car squeak as they are applied, the PROBABLE cause is the fact that the brake
   A. linings are dry
   B. linings are wet
   C. pedal is out of adjustment
   D. shoes are warped

   4.____

5. A compression test of all cylinders in an automobile engine is made PRIMARILY to
   A. check uniformity among the cylinders
   B. obtain the highest reading possible
   C. check on the specified compression ratio
   D. check the cylinder bore condition

   5.____

6. Valve springs are used to
   A. open the valves
   B. keep the valves open
   C. open and close the valves
   D. close the valves

   6.____

7. A common cause of an over-rich carburetor mixture is a
   A. dirty air cleaner
   B. leaking intake valve in the fuel pump
   C. low float level in the carburetor
   D. late spark timing

   7.____

8. The pin that transmits power from the piston to the connecting rod is called the _____ pin.
   A. king
   B. wrist
   C. connecting rod
   D. taper

9. Spark plugs that foul because of excessive carbon formation produced by slow speed engine operation can be corrected by
   A. installing spark plugs of a higher heat range
   B. advancing the ignition timing
   C. lowering the carburetor fuel level
   D. adjusting the manifold heat control valve

10. In a six-cylinder engine, the cranks on the crankshaft are set apart _____ degrees.
    A. 30
    B. 45
    C. 120
    D. 60

11. A carburetor that causes hard starting when the engine is hot may be corrected by
    A. the installation of an accelerator pump piston
    B. an anti-percolating valve
    C. installing a new high speed jet
    D. adjustment of the throttle valve set screw

12. A dragging of the brakes at one wheel may be caused by
    A. excessive grease on the lining
    B. a clogged brake line
    C. insufficient fluid in the master cylinder
    D. a leaking wheel cylinder

13. Toe-in of front wheels is necessary to
    A. offset the drag created by the caster angle
    B. compensate for the decrease in the king pin inclination
    C. produce easy recovery to a straight ahead position after turning a corner
    D. overcome the run-out due to the camber angle

14. A manifold heat control valve that is sticking in the *open* position will cause
    A. sluggish engine operation when cold
    B. hard starting when the engine is hot
    C. vapor lock
    D. a substantial increase in fuel consumption

15. A vacuum gauge shows a normal engine condition when
    A. the reading indicates a fluctuation between 15 and 17 inches of mercury
    B. there is a steady reading of 17 to 21 inches of mercury
    C. there is an intermittent reading of 16 to 18 inches of mercury
    D. there is a steady reading of 16 inches of mercury

16. A cam ground piston means that it
    A. is elliptical in shape
    B. uses no piston rings
    C. has no wrist pin
    D. has a complex head formation

17. Accurate spacing of the distributor points is accomplished with the use of a
    A. flat thickness gauge
    B. round thickness gauge
    C. syncroscope
    D. dial indicator

18. Hydraulic brake liquid leaking at the rubber boot at the end of a master cylinder USUALLY indicates
    A. a faulty check valve
    B. that the master cylinder has been overfilled
    C. leakage at the primary cup
    D. leakage at the master cylinder cup washer

19. Light detonation or spark knock that occurs when accelerating with a fully opened throttle on a hard pull indicates that
    A. the spark is too far advanced
    B. the spark is too far retarded
    C. the condition is normal
    D. a low grade of fuel is being used

20. Breaker points in service for some time may appear dull and gray upon inspection. This condition is
    A. due to a high battery voltage
    B. due to improper condenser capacity
    C. a normal condition
    D. due to a high resistance in the primary circuit

21. When a conventional automobile transmission is in neutral position, with the clutch engaged and the engine running,
    A. both the countershaft and the clutch shaft are turning
    B. only the countershaft is turning
    C. only the clutch shaft is turning
    D. only the reverse idler shaft is turning

22. The condenser in the electrical system of an automobile is used to
    A. increase the spark at the distributor points
    B. retard the ignition timing
    C. reduce arcing at the breaker points
    D. complete the primary circuit

23. Positive camber in the front wheels tends to
    A. overcome the effect of *toe-in*
    B. overcome the effect of *toe-out*
    C. overcome the effect of caster
    D. center the weight of the vehicle on the large inner wheel cearing

24. Hypoid rear ends should be lubricated with a(n)
    A. aluminum soap grease
    B. fibrous grease
    C. low pressure lubricant
    D. extreme pressure lubricant

25. The MAIN advantage of hydraulic brake systems is that they
    A. do not wear out the linings as rapidly as mechanical brakes do
    B. apply uniform pressure to each set of wheel brakes
    C. stop the automobile more quickly
    D. do not require adjustment

26. The purpose of an overdrive unit on automobile is to
    A. increase the speed of an engine in relation to the speed of the wheels
    B. simplify shifting
    C. increase the speed of the wheels in relation to the speed of the engine
    D. aid in braking the speed of the car when descending hills

27. The S.A.E. number of a lubricant indicates its
    A. tar content   B. flash point
    C. viscosity   D. acid content

28. *Hot, cold,* or *standard* spark plugs are distinguished by the
    A. shape and length of the lower porcelain insulator
    B. overall length of the plug
    C. diameter of the shell
    D. thickness of the shell

29. The amount of fuel mixture that can be drawn into a cylinder depends upon the
    A. displacement of the piston   B. combustion chamber area
    C. spark timing   D. speed of the fuel pump

30. To adjust the valves of an automobile engine, it is necessary to have the piston on
    A. bottom dead center
    B. top dead center
    C. intake stroke
    D. top dead center compression stroke

31. The backing plate on all automobiles is used PRIMARILY to
    A. retain the axle in the housing
    B. keep water from entering the brake mechanism
    C. provide a support for the brake shoes
    D. aid in stopping the automobile

32. The Hotchkiss type of rear-end drive uses
    A. two radius rods, sometimes attached to the front ends of the rear housing and to the upper face of the car's frame
    B. the two rear springs to absorb the rear-end torque and to transmit the driving thrust to the frame of the car
    C. two angle irons shaped like the letter *V*, reinforced with a cross rod
    D. a metal casing around the driveshaft

33. The camshaft of a four-stroke cycle engine rotates at 33.____
    A. crankshaft speed   B. one-half crankshaft speed
    C. one-quarter crankshaft speed   D. twice crankshaft speed

34. Looking in the direction in which a current flow through a conductor, the 34.____
    magnetic field surrounding it always travels in a(n) _____ direction.
    A. alternating   B. anti-clockwise
    C. southerly   D. clockwise

35. Contact point spring pressure should be set at _____ ounces 35.____
    A. 6 to 10   B. 17 to 21   C. 31 to 35   D. 36 to 40

36. The resistance of a suppressor may be measured by a(n) 36.____
    A. voltmeter   B. ohmmeter
    C. watt meter   D. inductance meter

37. The capacity of a condenser is generally measured in 37.____
    A. microfarads   B. farads   C. milliamps   D. ohms

38. Breaker points of a six cylinder engine should be set at 38.____
    A. .018   B. .0018   C. .180   D. 1.80

39. A fuse is placed in the lighting circuit to prevent 39.____
    A. short circuit   B. horn from blowing
    C. damage to wiring   D. overload of generator

40. The voltage of a battery is determined by 40.____
    A. the number of plates in each cell
    B. adding a stronger acid solution to the electrolyte
    C. connecting more cells in parallel
    D. connecting more cells in series

41. The blood vessels that carry blood toward the heart are the 41.____
    A. arteries   B. capillaries   C. corpuscles   D. veins

42. If an artery has been cut, you could tell by the 42.____
    A. quick clotting of the blood   B. Rh factor of the blood
    C. slow, steady flow of blood   D. spurting of the blood

43. The BEST material to be used directly over a wound or burn is 43.____
    A. absorbent cotton   B. adhesive tape
    C. sterile gauze   D. a tourniquet

44. Aromatic spirits of ammonia is used as a(n) 44.____
    A. antidote for arsenic poisoning   B. stimulant
    C. sedative drug   D. sterilizing solution

45. A compound fracture is one in which   45._____
    A. broken bones protrude through the skin
    B. bones are broken and shattered
    C. a large bone and its adjoining smaller bones are broken
    D. two or more bones are broken

Questions 46-50.

DIRECTIONS: Each of Questions 46 through 50 consists of a group of four words. Examine each group carefully, then in the space at the right print the letter
A if only one word in the group is spelled correctly
B if two words in the group are spelled correctly
C if three words in the group are spelled correctly
D if all four words in the group are spelled correctly

46. Wendsday, particular, similar, hunderd   46._____

47. realize, judgment, opportunities, consistent   47._____

48. equel, principle, assistense, commitee   48._____

49. simultaneous, privilege, advise, ocassionaly   49._____

50. necissery, official, Febuary, distence

KEY (CORRECT ANSWERS)

1.	B	11.	B	21.	A	31.	C	41.	D
2.	C	12.	B	22.	C	32.	B	42.	D
3.	C	13.	D	23.	D	33.	B	43.	C
4.	D	14.	A	24.	D	34.	D	44.	B
5.	A	15.	B	25.	B	35.	B	45.	A
6.	D	16.	A	26.	C	36.	B	46.	B
7.	A	17.	D	27.	C	37.	A	47.	D
8.	B	18.	D	28.	A	38.	A	48.	A
9.	A	19.	C	29.	A	39.	C	49.	C
10.	C	20.	C	30.	D	40.	D	50.	A

TEST 2

DIRECTIONS: Each question consists of a statement. You are to indicate whether the statement is TRUE (T) or FALSE (F). *PRINT THE LETTER OF THE CORRECT ANSWER IN THE SPACE AT THE RIGHT.*

1. The starting of an engine is NOT affected by a sticking automatic choke. 1.____

2. To aid the starting of an overchoked engine, it is necessary to crank the engine with the throttle wide open to help clear the cylinders of raw gasoline. 2.____

3. The oil pressure gauge indicates the quantity of oil in the crankcase. 3.____

4. A lighter grade of oil should be used during cold weather driving. 4.____

5. The purpose of the cooling fan is to help dissipate the heat from the cylinder block. 5.____

6. The generator is a device which converts mechanical energy into electrical energy. 6.____

7. A shunt generator without a voltage regulator will not tend to increase the voltage output with the increase in the engine speed. 7.____

8. The output of a third brush generator is increased by moving the third brush away from the main brush. 8.____

9. The cut-out relay prevents the battery from discharging through the generator when the engine is stopped. 9.____

10. The coil in an ignition system is used to build up a high voltage in the primary circuit. 10.____

11. To check the condition of a storage batter, it is only necessary to check the specific gravity of the acid in the storage battery. 11.____

12. A specific gravity reading of 1.100 indicates a battery in full charge condition. 12.____

13. When the battery acid reading varies between the cells of a storage battery, it is only necessary to add stronger acid to the weak cells. 13.____

14. Distributor rotor shafts always rotate in a clockwise direction. 14.____

15. A good spark at the spark plug depends entirely on the charge condition of the storage battery. 15.____

16. The condenser helps to quench the spark at the breaker points. 16.____

17. Breaker points will burn away rapidly if the cam angle is too great. 17.____

79

18. If the lights dim considerably when the starting motor is operated, this indicates a faulty ground connection. 18.____

19. Increasing temperatures cause oil to gain body and lose fluidity, while decreasing temperatures cause oil to lose body and gain fluidity. 19.____

20. In a splash lubricating system, the oil is pumped under pressure to all working parts of the engine. 20.____

21. An over-rich carburetor mixture is indicated by a white smoke emitted from the exhaust pipe. 21.____

22. When an engine stalls after a violent braking of the vehicle, it indicates that the carburetor idling mixture is too lean. 22.____

23. High speed duel supply depends entirely on the idling jet in the carburetor. 23.____

24. The accelerator pump injects a supply of gasoline to the manifold when the throttle is opened suddenly. 24.____

25. To pressure flush a radiator, it is proper to exert a pressure at the top of the core to force the clogged material out of the bottom of the core. 25.____

26. An engine water thermostat is provided to restrict water circulation when the engine is cold. 26.____

27. Corrosion of the radiator and parts of the cooling system may be caused by exhaust gas leaking into the cooling system through a defective cylinder head gasket. 27.____

28. An L-head type of engine is one in which the intake valves are located on one side of the engine block and the exhaust valves are located on the other side of the engine block. 28.____

29. A worn valve guide will cause excessive oil consumption. 29.____

30. Counterweights on crankshafts are provided to compensate for the weight of the flywheel. 30.____

31. Worn main bearings will produce a typical crankshaft knock that is especially noticeable when the engine is under a hard pull. 31.____

32. An oil wiper ring on a piston is a device that insures proper lubrication to the cylinder walls. 32.____

33. The order in which the events of a four-stroke cycle occur is: 1 – compression, 2 – intake, 3 – power, 4 – exhaust. 33.____

34. Fuels for gasoline engines are rated according to octane number, those having the higher octane rating are those having the GREATEST tendency to knock.

34._____

35. An efficient combustible mixture for a gasoline engine is one part of gasoline to fifteen parts of air by volume.

35._____

36. A loose piston pin will indicate itself by a double knock MOSTLY noticeable during idling.

36._____

37. The operation of a clutch is based on the frictional contact between two smooth metallic surfaces and the facings riveted to the friction disk.

37._____

38. A slipping clutch may be caused by the lack of free clutch pedal action.

38._____

39. Hydraulic transmissions are operated by the vacuum produced in the engine intake manifold.

39._____

40. A chattering clutch may be caused by oil or gum on the pressure plate, friction disk, or flywheel facing.

40._____

41. A dragging clutch may be caused by a warped or distorted pressure plate.

41._____

42. Syncro mesh devices are designed to cause gear that are rotating and about to be meshed to rotate at the same speeds so that meshing can take place easily.

42._____

43. In constant mesh type transmissions, the gears are moved to become engaged or disengaged according to the need.

43._____

44. The vacuum or power gear shift uses intake manifold vacuum to provide the needed power to shift gears.

44._____

45. The overdrive unit reduces engine speed for high car speeds, providing more economical operation and less engine wear per car mile.

45._____

46. Hard gear shifting may be caused by sliding gears being tight on the splined shaft.

46._____

47. The proper shaft universal joints are provided to allow for the difference in shaft positions when the wheels ride over a bump.

47._____

48. A differential is required to compensate for the difference in distances the rear wheels travel when the car rounds a turn.

48._____

49. In the semi-floating type of rear axle, the wheel end of the axle shaft is supported by a bearing in the axle housing.

49._____

50. A leaf spring has a slower rate of vibration than a coil spring, thereby giving a much easier ride.   50.____

KEY (CORRECT ANSWERS)

1.	F	11.	F	21.	F	31.	T	41.	T
2.	T	12.	F	22.	T	32.	F	42.	T
3.	F	13.	F	23.	F	33.	F	43.	F
4.	T	14.	F	24.	T	34.	F	44.	T
5.	T	15.	F	25.	F	35.	F	45.	T
6.	T	16.	T	26.	T	36.	T	46.	T
7.	F	17.	T	27.	T	37.	T	47.	T
8.	F	18.	F	28.	F	38.	T	48.	T
9.	T	19.	F	29.	T	39.	F	49.	T
10.	F	20.	F	30.	F	40.	T	50.	F

TEST 3

DIRECTIONS: Each question consists of a statement. You are to indicate whether the statement is TRUE (T) or FALSE (F). *PRINT THE LETTER OF THE CORRECT ANSWER IN THE SPACE AT THE RIGHT.*

1. A weak front spring of the leaf type may cause a change in the caster effect. 1.____

2. Shock absorbers are provided to overcome the violent rebound action after a spring has been compressed. 2.____

3. The hydraulic type of shock absorber depends upon the difference of air pressure within the unit for its efficient operation. 3.____

4. Caster effect is put into a front axle by tilting the upper parts of the king pin towards the front of the car. 4.____

5. Excessive caster effect will cause the wheels to shimmy. 5.____

6. On modern vehicles, the camber effect is kept at a minimum due to the king pin inclination. 6.____

7. Excessive camber may cause tire wear at the outer edge of the tire. 7.____

8. Scuffing of the tire surface may be caused by a bent steering arm. 8.____

9. The pitman arm is the connecting link between the steering gear assembly and the drag link. 9.____

10. The reach rod connects the front wheels with the steering column. 10.____

11. Steering arms must be positioned to give proper toe-in when the car is on a turn. 11.____

12. If a car persistently pulls to one side, this may be caused by low or uneven tire pressures. 12.____

13. Steering gears are provided with adjustments to eliminate end play in the cross shaft and worm and wheel contact. 13.____

14. A properly adjusted steering gear will be indicated by a slight drag at the center position and free action at the extreme end positions. 14.____

15. When checking for caster, camber, or toe-in, it is necessary to have the car in a level position and the tires inflated to the proper pressures. 15.____

16. The effectiveness of hydraulic brakes is based upon the principle that hydraulic pressure is exerted equally in all directions in a liquid under pressure. 16.____

17. Noisy or squealing brakes may be caused by loose linings or rivets that touch the brake drum. 17.____

18. When all brakes drag on a car equipped with a hydraulic system, this condition may be caused by a clogged filler vent on the master cylinder. 18.____

19. Air in the hydraulic brake lines indicates the necessity for bleeding the entire brake system. 19.____

20. Piston displacement is the volume that the piston displaces as it moves from top dead center to bottom dead center position. 20.____

21. The stroke of an engine is the distance the piston travels from top dead center to bottom dead center 21.____

22. Low pressure in a full force lubrication system may indicate loose bearings. 22.____

23. A cracked distributor cap may cause a miss in the engine. 23.____

24. The S.A.E. number of lubricating oils indicates the degree of viscosity of the oil. 24.____

25. Vapor lock will NOT affect the running of an engine. 25.____

26. Late spark timing will cause an engine to overheat. 26.____

27. Excessive pressure in air brake systems may be caused by sticking relief valves. 27.____

28. A magneto depends upon a battery for a current to operate the breaker system. 28.____

29. The intensity of a spark produced by a magneto depends upon the speed of the magneto armature. 29.____

30. The camshaft of an engine rotates at one-half the speed of the crankshaft. 30.____

31. A battery that is badly sulphated may be corrected by placing the battery on a low charge for a long period of time. 31.____

32. A voltage regulator controls the voltage output of the battery. 32.____

33. Rebound clips on leaf springs are provided to prevent the spring from shifting on the spring saddle. 33.____

34. The fuel pump that delivers gasoline to the carburetor does so under pressure. 34.____

35. A high float level in the carburetor may cause an over-rich operating condition. 35.____

36. Crankcase ventilation is provided to help carry off the vapors of water and gasoline when the engine reaches operating temperature. 36.____

37. The pressure cap allows circulation of water in the cooling system at higher temperatures without boiling. 37.____

38. Excessive fuel consumption may be caused by underinflated tires. 38.____

39. Accelerator pump linkage control must be adjusted for winter and for summer driving. 39.____

40. Excessive oil consumption may be caused by a broken oil seal at the rear main bearing. 40.___

41. If a battery is allowed to stand for a long period of time, it will slowly self-discharge. 41.____

42. If the battery requires a considerable amount of water, it indicates that the charge rate is too low. 42.____

43. It is advisable to coat the battery terminals with petroleum jelly to prevent corrosion. 43.____

44. A low or unsteady output from a generator may be caused by a round, dirty, or worn commutator. 44.____

45. Valve tappet noise may be caused by excessive clearance between the valve stem and the valve guide. 45.____

46. A slipping clutch is caused by excessive pressure of the pressure springs. 46.____

47. The transmission interlocking device is provided to prevent the shifting of more than one gear at a time. 47.____

48. High speed driving will not wear tires more than slow speed driving. 48.____

49. High speed driving on hot pavements will cause a rise in pressure in the tire. 49.____

50. Spark plug gaps must be varied according to the compression ratio of the engine. 50.____

KEY (CORRECT ANSWERS)

1. T	11. F	21. T	31. T	41. T
2. T	12. T	22. T	32. F	42. F
3. F	13. T	23. T	33. F	43. T
4. F	14. T	24. T	34. T	44. T
5. T	15. T	25. F	35. T	45. F
6. T	16. T	26. T	36. T	46. F
7. T	17. T	27. T	37. T	47. T
8. T	18. T	28. F	38. T	48. F
9. T	19. T	29. T	39. T	49. T
10. F	20. T	30. T	40. T	50. F

EXAMINATION SECTION
TEST 1

DIRECTIONS: Each question or incomplete statement is followed by several suggested answers or completions. Select the one that BEST answers the question or completes the statement. *PRINT THE LETTER OF THE CORRECT ANSWER IN THE SPACE AT THE RIGHT.*

1. Of the following, the one that is a grease fitting is a _____ fitting. 1._____

   A. Morse
   B. Brown and Sharpe
   C. Zerk
   D. caliper

2. In an automobile equipped with an ammeter, the ammeter is used to 2._____

   A. indicate current flow
   B. regulate current flow
   C. act as a circuit breaker
   D. measure engine r.p.m.

3. The ignition points in the distributor of a gasoline engine are opened by means of a 3._____

   A. spring
   B. vacuum
   C. cam with lobes
   D. gear

4. MOST automobile engines that use gasoline as fuel operate as _____ engines. 4._____

   A. single cycle
   B. single stroke, single cycle
   C. two-stroke, two-cycle
   D. four-stroke, two-cycle

5. For a shop manager, the MOST important reason that equipment which is used infrequently should be considered for disposal is that 5._____

   A. such equipment may cause higher management to think that your shop is not busy
   B. the time required for its maintenance could be better used elsewhere
   C. the men may resent having to work on such equipment
   D. such equipment usually has a higher breakdown rate in operation

6. The PRIMARY function of the thermostat in the cooling system of an automobile engine is to 6._____

   A. control the operating temperature of the engine
   B. keep the operating temperature of the engine as low as possible
   C. provide the proper amount of heat for the heater
   D. retain engine heat when the engine gets hot

7. The PRIMARY purpose of the condenser in the ignition circuit of a gasoline engine is to 7._____

   A. boost the ignition voltage
   B. rectify the ignition voltage
   C. adjust the coil voltage
   D. reduce arcing at the distributor breaker points

8. The PRIMARY purpose of the differential in the rear drive train of an automotive vehicle is to allow each of the rear wheels to

   A. rotate at different speeds
   B. go in reverse
   C. rotate with maximum torque
   D. absorb road shocks

9. When an automobile engine does not start on a damp day, the trouble is MOST likely in the _____ system.

   A. ignition
   B. cooling
   C. fuel
   D. lubricating

10. The battery of an automobile is prevented from discharging back through the alternator by the blocking action of the

    A. commutator
    B. diodes
    C. brushes
    D. slip rings

11. The master cylinder in an automobile is actuated by the

    A. steering column
    B. brake pedal
    C. clutch plate
    D. cam shaft

Questions 12-17.

DIRECTIONS: Questions 12 through 17 are to be answered SOLELY on the basis of the following passage.

The basic hand-operated hoisting device is the tackle or purchase, consisting of a line called a fall, reeved through one or more blocks.

To hoist a load of given size, you must set up a rig with a safe working load equal to or in excess of the load to be hoisted. In order to do this, you must be able to calculate the safe working load of a single part of line of given size; the safe working load of a given purchase which contains a line of given size; and the minimum size of hooks or shackles which you must use in a given type of purchase to hoist a given load. You must also be able to calculate the thrust which a given load will exert on a gin pole or a set of shears inclined at a given angle; the safe working load which a spar of a given size, used as a gin pole or as one of a set of shears, will sustain; and the stress which a given load will set up in the back guy of a gin pole, or in the back guy of a set of shears, inclined at a given angle.

12. The above passage refers to the lifting of loads by means of

    A. erected scaffolds
    B. manual rigging devices
    C. power-driven equipment
    D. conveyor belts

13. It can be concluded from the above passage that a set of shears serves to

    A. absorb the force and stress of the working load
    B. operate the tackle
    C. contain the working load
    D. compute the safe working load

14. According to the above passage, a spar can be used for a 14.____

    A. back guy   B. block   C. fall   D. gin pole

15. According to the above passage, the rule that a user of hand-operated tackle MUST follow is to make sure that the safe working load is AT LEAST 15.____

    A. equal to the weight of the given load
    B. twice the combined weight of the block and falls
    C. one-half the weight of the given load
    D. twice the weight of the given load

16. According to the above passage, the two parts that make up a tackle are 16.____

    A. back guys and gin poles   B. blocks and falls
    C. rigs and shears   D. spars and shackle

17. According to the above passage, in order to determine whether it is safe to hoist a particular load, you MUST 17.____

    A. use the maximum size hooks
    B. time the speed to bring a given load to a desired place
    C. calculate the forces exerted on various types of rigs
    D. repeatedly lift and lower various loads

18. If you do not understand the operation of some special tool which is used in your work, your BEST procedure would be to 18.____

    A. study up on its operation at home
    B. ask a maintainer to explain its operation
    C. ask another helper to explain its operation
    D. bother nobody and expect to pick up a little more knowledge each time you use the tool

19. For winter servicing of a gasoline engine, it is BEST to use an oil that 19.____

    A. has a low SAE number
    B. has a high SAE number
    C. has a very heavy consistency
    D. contains few additive detergents

20. If a wheel has turned through an angle of 180°, then it has made _____ revolution(s). 20.____

    A. 1/4   B. 1/2   C. 1/8   D. 18

21. The crankshaft in a gasoline engine is PRIMARILY used to 21.____

    A. change reciprocating motion to rotary motion
    B. operate the valve lifters
    C. supply power to each cylinder
    D. function as a flywheel

22. Assume that a mechanic is using a powder-actuated tool and the cartridge misfires. According to recommended safe practices regarding a misfired cartridge, the FIRST course of action the mechanic should take is to

   A. place the misfired cartridge carefully into a metal container filled with water
   B. carefully reload the tool with the misfired cartridge and try it again
   C. immediately bury the misfired cartridge at least two feet in the ground
   D. remove the wadding from the misfired cartridge and empty the powder into a pail of sand

23. The purpose of the ignition coil in a gasoline engine is PRIMARILY to

   A. smooth the voltage
   B. raise the voltage
   C. raise the current
   D. smooth the current

24. Vapor lock in a vehicle with a gasoline engine is caused by excessive heat. To prevent vapor lock, it may be necessary to relocate

   A. the ignition system
   B. the cooling system
   C. the starter motor
   D. a part of the fuel line

25. To accurately measure the small gap between relay contacts, it is BEST to use a(n)

   A. depth gauge
   B. *GO-NO GO* gauge
   C. feeler gauge
   D. inside caliper

KEY (CORRECT ANSWERS)

1.	C	11.	B
2.	A	12.	B
3.	C	13.	A
4.	D	14.	D
5.	B	15.	A
6.	A	16.	B
7.	D	17.	C
8.	A	18.	B
9.	A	19.	A
10.	B	20.	B

21.	A
22.	A
23.	B
24.	D
25.	C

TEST 2

DIRECTIONS: Each question or incomplete statement is followed by several suggested answers or completions. Select the one that BEST answers the question or completes the statement. *PRINT THE LETTER OF THE CORRECT ANSWER IN THE SPACE AT THE RIGHT.*

1. Of the following, the MOST important reason for having a vehicle preventive maintenance and history card is   1.____

    A. for use in making vehicle assignments
    B. to check whether the drivers are completing their assignments
    C. for use as a control device in scheduling maintenance
    D. as a means for projecting future maintenance expenses

2. In his efforts to maintain standards of performance, a shop manager uses a system of close supervision to detect or catch errors.   2.____
In OPPOSITE method of accomplishing the same objective is to employ a program which

    A. instills in each employee a pride of workmanship to do the job correctly the first time
    B. groups each job according to the importance to the overall objectives of the program
    C. makes the control of quality the responsibility of an inspector
    D. emphasizes that there is a *one* best way for an employee to do a specific job

3. Assume that after taking over a repair shop, a shop manager feels that he is taking too much time maintaining records.   3.____
He should

    A. temporarily assign this job to one of his senior repair crew chiefs
    B. get together with his supervisor to determine if all these records are needed
    C. stop keeping those records which he believes are unnecessary
    D. spend a few additional hours each day until his records are current

4. In order to apply performance standards to employees engaged in repair shop activities, a shop manager must FIRST   4.____

    A. allow workers to decide for themselves the way to do the job
    B. determine what is acceptable as satisfactory work
    C. separate the more difficult tasks from the simpler tasks
    D. stick to an established work schedule

5. The term *preventative maintenance* is used to identify a plan whereby   5.____

    A. equipment is serviced according to a regular schedule
    B. equipment is serviced as soon as it fails
    C. equipment is replaced as soon as it becomes obsolete
    D. all equipment is replaced periodically

91

6. The ratio of air to gasoline in an automobile engine is controlled by the 6.____

    A. gas filter   B. fuel pump
    C. fuel injector   D. intake manifold

7. *Energizer* is another name given to the 7.____

    A. automobile battery
    B. fluorescent fixture ballast
    C. battery charger
    D. generator shunt field

8. Wearshoes may be found on 8.____

    A. circuit breakers   B. automobile brake systems
    C. snow plows   D. door sills

9. An oscilloscope is an instrument used in 9.____

    A. measuring noise levels
    B. displaying waveforms of electrical signals
    C. indicating the concentrations of pollutants in air
    D. photographing high-speed events

10. Assume that a brake pedal of a truck goes to the floorboard when depressed. The one of the following that could cause this condition Is 10.____

    A. a leak in the hydraulic lines
    B. a clogged hydraulic line
    C. scored drums
    D. glazed linings

11. The universal joints of an automobile are located on the 11.____

    A. suspension springs   B. steering linkages
    C. wheel cylinders   D. drive shaft

12. The MAIN purpose of a flexible coupling is to connect two shafts which are 12.____

    A. of different diameters   B. of different shapes
    C. not in exact alignment   D. of different material

13. When using a standard measuring micrometer, starting with a zero reading, one complete counterclockwise revolution of the sleeve will give a reading of _____ inch. 13.____

    A. .001   B. .010   C. .025   D. .250

14. If a nut is to be tightened to an exact specified value of inch-lbs., the wrench to use is a _____ wrench. 14.____

    A. spanner   B. box   C. lock-jaw   D. torque

15. Common permanent type anti-freezes for automobile cooling systems are MAINLY 15.____

    A. alcohol   B. methanol
    C. ethylene glycol   D. trichloroethylene

16. The function of the fuel injector on a gasoline engine is to

    A. mix the air and gasoline properly
    B. filter the fuel
    C. filter the air to engine
    D. pump the gasoline into the cylinder

17. If a car owner complains that the battery in his car is constantly running dry, the item that should be checked FIRST is the

    A. fan belt
    B. generator
    C. voltage regulator
    D. relay

18. On MOST modern automobiles, foot brake pressure is transmitted to the brake drums by

    A. air pressure
    B. mechanical linkage
    C. hydraulic fluid
    D. electromagnetic force

19. Assume that the engine of a car remains cold even though it is run for a period of time. The part that is MOST likely at fault is the

    A. heat bypass valve
    B. thermostat
    C. heater control
    D. choke

20. A rectifier changes

    A. DC to AC
    B. AC to DC
    C. single-phase power to three-phase power
    D. battery power to three-phase power

21. Continuity in a de-energized electrical circuit may be checked with a(n)

    A. voltmeter
    B. ohmmeter
    C. neon tester
    D. rheostat

22. Of the following crankcase oils, the one that should be used in sub-zero weather is SAE

    A. 10W   B. 20W   C. 20   D. 30

23. Caster in an automobile is an adjustment in the

    A. ignition system
    B. drive-shaft
    C. rear differential
    D. front suspension

24. If the spark plugs in an engine run too hot, the result is MOST likely that

    A. oil and carbon compounds will accumulate on the insulators
    B. the electrodes will wear rapidly
    C. the timing will be retarded
    D. the ignition coil may become damaged

25. A low reading on the oil pressure gauge of a gasoline engine may mean that the   25.____
    A. engine bearings are too tight
    B. crankcase oil level is too low
    C. transmission oil level is too low
    D. transmission oil needs changing

KEY (CORRECT ANSWERS)

1. C
2. A
3. B
4. B
5. A

6. C
7. A
8. C
9. B
10. A

11. D
12. C
13. C
14. D
15. C

16. A
17. C
18. C
19. B
20. B

21. B
22. A
23. D
24. B
25. B

TEST 3

DIRECTIONS: Each question or incomplete statement is followed by several suggested answers or completions. Select the one that BEST answers the question or completes the statement. *PRINT THE LETTER OF THE CORRECT ANSWER IN THE SPACE AT THE RIGHT.*

1. To remove a slotted collar having internal threads from a shaft, the BEST of the following wrenches to use is a(n) _____ wrench.

    A. Allen   B. Stillson   C. socket   D. spanner

2. When using a heavy jack placed on the ground to raise a heavy load, it is important to place a sturdy, flat board under the jack PRIMARILY in order to

    A. facilitate placing the jack under the load
    B. reduce the jacking effort
    C. prevent the jack from slipping out from under the load
    D. decrease the jacking height

3. The pulley wheels of a block and tackle are commonly called

    A. stocks   B. swivels   C. sheaves   D. guides

4. If the diameter of a machined part must be 1.035 ± 0.003", then it is ACCEPTABLE if it measures

    A. 1.031"   B. 1.032"   C. 1.039"   D. 1.335"

5. The type of threads for ordinary screws are USUALLY the _____ type.

    A. square   B. buttress   C. V   D. Acme

6. Of the following actions a repair shop manager can take to determine if the vehicles used in his shop are being utilized properly, the one which will give him the LEAST meaningful information is

    A. conducting an analysis of vehicle assignments
    B. reviewing the number of miles travelled by each vehicle with and without loads
    C. recording the unloaded weights of each vehicle
    D. comparing the amount of time vehicles are parked at job sites with the time required to travel to and from job sites

7. For a shop manager, the MOST important reason that equipment which is used infrequently should be considered for disposal is that

    A. the time required for its maintenance could be better used elsewhere
    B. such equipment may cause higher management to think that your shop is not busy
    C. the men may resent having to work on such equipment
    D. such equipment usually has a higher breakdown rate in operation

8. In an automotive gasoline engine, the camshaft is used PRIMARILY to

    A. drive the transmission
    B. operate the valve lifters
    C. change the reciprocating motion of the pistons to rotary motion
    D. operate the choke mechanism

9. A magnetic motor starter is to be controlled with momentary start-stop pushbuttons at two locations.
    The number of control wires required, respectively, in the conduit between the controller and the first station and in the conduit between the two stations is _____ and _____.

    A. 3; 3   B. 4; 4   C. 3; 4   D. 2; 4

10. If the scale on a shop drawing is 1/2 inch to the foot, then the length of a part which measures 4 1/2 inches long on the drawing has a length of APPROXIMATELY _____ feet.

    A. 2 1/8   B. 4 1/4   C. 8 1/2   D. 10 3/4

11. It is important to use safety shoes PRIMARILY to guard the feet against

    A. tripping hazards   B. heavy falling objects
    C. shock hazards   D. mud and dirt

12. When using a wrench to tighten a bolt, it is considered bad practice to extend the handle of the wrench with a pipe for added leverage PRIMARILY because

    A. the pipe may break
    B. the bolt head may be broken off
    C. more space will be needed to turn the wrench with the pipe on it
    D. no increase in leverage is obtained in this manner

13. The liquid solution in an electrical storage battery MOST commonly is

    A. alkali   B. acid
    C. pure distilled water   D. copper sulphate

14. Manifolds on an internal combustion engine are used

    A. to mount the engine to the frame
    B. for cooling the engine
    C. in the carburetor
    D. to conduct gases into and out of the engine

15. The energy stored by a storage battery is commonly given in

    A. volts   B. amperes
    C. ampere-hours   D. kilowatts

16. Vapor lock occurs in automobile

    A. gas tanks   B. crankcases
    C. transmissions   D. carburetors

17. The instrument generally used to determine the specific gravity of a lead-acid storage battery is the

    A. ammeter
    B. voltmeter
    C. ohmmeter
    D. hydrometer

18. A tachometer is an instrument that is used to measure

    A. horizontal distances
    B. radial distances
    C. current in electric circuits
    D. motor speed

19. A material that is commonly used as a lining for bearings in order to reduce friction is

    A. magnesium
    B. cast iron
    C. babbitt
    D. carborundum

20. In a motor having sleeve bearings, bearing wear can be checked by measuring the air-gap clearance between the armature and the

    A. pole pieces
    B. commutator
    C. bearing
    D. brushes

21. A revolution counter applied to the end of a rotating shaft reads 100 when a stopwatch is started and 850 after 90 seconds.
    The shaft is rotating at a speed of _____ rpm.

    A. 500
    B. 633
    C. 750
    D. 950

22. If a kink develops in a wire rope, it would be BEST to

    A. hammer out the kink with a lead hammer
    B. straighten out the kink by putting it in a vise and applying sufficient pressure
    C. discard the portion of rope containing the kink
    D. keep the rope in use and allow the kink to work itself out

23. The one of the following flat drive-belts that gives the BEST service in dry places is a(n) _____ belt.

    A. rawhide
    B. oak-tanned
    C. chrome-tanned
    D. semirawhide

24. The letter representing the standard V-belt section which has the lowest horsepower-per-belt rating is

    A. E
    B. C
    C. B
    D. A

25. The criteria governing preventive maintenance of vehicles require that all of the following be done at certain intervals.
    The one which must be done MOST frequently is

    A. changing the engine oil
    B. changing the engine oil filter
    C. checking the radiator coolant level
    D. rotating the tires

26. The one of the following that should NOT be lubricated is a(n)

    A. spur gear train B. motor commutator
    C. roller chain drive D. automobile axle

27. The one of the following oils that has the LOWEST viscosity is S.A.E.

    A. 70   B. 50   C. 20   D. 10W

28. The one of the following V-belt sections which has the HIGHEST horsepower-per-belt rating is _____ section.

    A. A   B. B   C. C   D. D

29. The one of the following transmission devices which should be oiled MOST often is the

    A. V-belt B. roller chain
    C. rigid coupling D. clutch plate

30. The one of the following statements concerning lubricating oil which is CORRECT is:

    A. SAE 10 is heavier and more viscous than SAE 30
    B. Diluting lubricating oil with gasoline increases its viscosity
    C. Oil reduces friction between moving parts
    D. In hot weather, thin oil is preferable to heavy oil

KEY (CORRECT ANSWERS)

1.	D	16.	D
2.	C	17.	D
3.	C	18.	D
4.	B	19.	C
5.	C	20.	A
6.	C	21.	A
7.	A	22.	C
8.	B	23.	B
9.	C	24.	D
10.	C	25.	C
11.	B	26.	B
12.	B	27.	D
13.	B	28.	D
14.	D	29.	B
15.	C	30.	C

EXAMINATION SECTION
TEST 1

DIRECTIONS: Each question or incomplete statement is followed by several suggested answers or completions. Select the one that BEST answers the question or completes the statement. *PRINT THE LETTER OF THE CORRECT ANSWER IN THE SPACE AT THE RIGHT.*

1. The practice of placing extra weight on the rear of a fork-lift truck which is carrying an overload is

    A. *undesirable*, because the operator has too much balancing to do
    B. *undesirable*, because it puts a strain on the motor, tires, and axle of the truck
    C. *desirable*, because this prevents the truck from turning over
    D. *desirable*, because more material can be transported at a time

2. Of the following, the MOST important reason for not letting oil rags accumulate in an open storage bin is that they

    A. may start a fire by spontaneous combustion
    B. will drip oil onto other items in the bin
    C. may cause a foul odor
    D. will make the area messy

3. The decimal equivalent of 5/64 is MOST NEARLY

    A. 0.065   B. 0.068   C. 0.075   D. 0.078

4. The sum of 3 1/2", 4 1/8", and 6 3/16" is

    A. 13 3/4"   B. 13 13/16"   C. 13 7/8"   D. 13 15/16"

5. Of the following, the BEST method to employ in putting out a gasoline fire is to

    A. use a bucket of water
    B. smother it with rags
    C. use a carbon dioxide extinguisher
    D. use a carbon tetrachloride extinguisher

6. Assume that you have to move ten 65-pound crates a distance of approximately 350 feet and each crate measures 14" x 26" x 32".
   From among the following methods, it would BEST to

    A. load the crates on a pallet and use a forklift truck
    B. carry one crate at a time by yourself
    C. load the crates on a skid and use pipe rollers to move the skid
    D. unpack each crate and move all of the contents with a motor van

7. Of the following, the BEST reason for stacking long rectangular tubes in layers, with the first layer lengthwise and the next layer crosswise, is that it

    A. reduces the overall stacking height
    B. makes it simpler to count the tubes

C. makes it easier to remove a tube from the center of the stack
D. prevents the stack of tubes from toppling

8. The ACCEPTED practice for a person to follow in lifting a heavy object off the floor is to

   A. keep both legs straight and close together, and to bend at the waist to grasp the object
   B. get a solid footing, and with both legs straight, bend at the waist and lift the object
   C. place the feet as far apart as possible and bend at the knees to reach down to grasp the object
   D. place the feet shoulder-width apart and bend at the knees to reach down to grasp the object

9. When a new shipment of material is received, it is sometimes necessary to store the new material in such a way that the old stock will be used first. It is MOST important to use this method with material that

   A. is ordered in large quantities
   B. is large in size
   C. is not used often
   D. deteriorates with age

10. If a certain type of material is packaged in a container which has written on it the words *Net weight 15 pounds,* it means that the _____ 15 pounds.

    A. material alone weighs
    B. container alone weighs
    C. material and the container together weigh
    D. capacity of the container is limited to

11. Of the following, the BEST reason for storing small items, such as nails, in their original containers whenever possible is that it

    A. makes it easier to inspect these items
    B. eliminates the need for bins and shelves
    C. makes it simpler to identify these items
    D. reduces the loss of the item due to theft

12. Of the following, the one that is a grease fitting is a _____ fitting.

    A. Brown   B. Zerk   C. Taper   D. Morse

13. Of the following, the BEST tool to use to make a hole in a concrete floor for a machine hold-down is a

    A. counterboring tool   B. cold chisel
    C. drift punch   D. star drill

14. Of the following, the BEST type of saw to use to cut a 4-inch diameter hole through a 5/8-inch wooden partition is a _____ saw.

    A. back   B. saber
    C. circular   D. cross-cut

15. When removing a shrink-fitted collar from a shaft, it would be EASIEST to drive out the shaft after

    A. heating only the collar
    B. heating only the shaft
    C. chilling only the collar
    D. chilling the collar and heating the shaft

15.____

16. Of the following, the BEST reason for overhauling a machine on a regular basis is

    A. that overhauling is easier to do when done often
    B. to minimize breakdowns of the machine
    C. to make sure the machine is properly lubricated
    D. to make sure the employees are familiar with the machine

16.____

17. While using a hacksaw to cut through a one-inch diameter steel bar, a helper should not press down too heavily on the hacksaw because this may

    A. break the blade
    B. overheat the bar
    C. permanently distort the frame
    D. cause the hacksaw to flip

17.____

18. A miter box is used

    A. for locating dowel holes in two pieces of wood to be joined together
    B. to hold a saw at a fixed angle while sawing
    C. to hold a saw while sharpening its teeth
    D. to clamp two pieces of wood together at 90 degrees

18.____

19. Wing nuts are ESPECIALLY useful on equipment where

    A. the nuts must be removed frequently and easily
    B. the nuts are locked in place with a cotter pin
    C. critical adjustments are to be made frequently
    D. a standard hex head wrench cannot be used

19.____

20. The BEST device to employ to make certain that two points, separated by an unobstructed vertical distance of 12 feet, are in the BEST possible vertical alignment is a

    A. carpenter's square
    B. level
    C. folding ruler
    D. plumb bob

20.____

21. In a shop, snips should be used to

    A. hold small parts steady while machining them
    B. cut threaded pipe
    C. cut thin gauge sheet metal
    D. remove nuts that are seized on a bolt

21.____

22. Caulking a joint means

    A. applying sealing material to the joint
    B. tightening the joint with wrenches
    C. opening it with wrenches
    D. testing the joint for leaks

22.____

23. When storing files, the MOST important reason for making sure that the files do not touch each other is to prevent

    A. damage to the file teeth
    B. damage to the file stands
    C. rusting of the files
    D. dirt from accumulating in the file teeth

24. A clutch is a device that is used

    A. to hold a work piece in a fixture
    B. for retrieving small parts from hard to reach areas
    C. to disengage one rotating shaft from another
    D. to level machinery on a floor

25. Of the following, the BEST device to use to determine whether the surface of a work bench is horizontal is a

    A. surface gage
    B. spirit level
    C. dial vernier
    D. profilometer

KEY (CORRECT ANSWERS)

1.	B	11.	C
2.	A	12.	B
3.	D	13.	D
4.	B	14.	B
5.	C	15.	A
6.	A	16.	B
7.	D	17.	A
8.	D	18.	B
9.	D	19.	A
10.	A	20.	D

21. C
22. A
23. A
24. C
25. B

TEST 2

DIRECTIONS: Each question or incomplete statement is followed by several suggested answers or completions. Select the one that BEST answers the question or completes the statement. *PRINT THE LETTER OF THE CORRECT ANSWER IN THE SPACE AT THE RIGHT.*

1. Of the following, the machine screw having the SMALLEST diameter is the

    A. 10-24 x 3/4"
    B. 6-32 x 1 1/4"
    C. 12-24 x 1"
    D. 8-32 x 1 1/2"

    1.____

2. When drilling into a steel plate, the MOST likely cause for the breaking of a drill bit is

    A. too low a drill speed
    B. excessive cutting oil lubricant
    C. too much drill pressure
    D. using a bit with a dull point

    2.____

3. Of the following, the MOST important advantage of a ratchet wrench over an open-end wrench is that the ratchet wrench

    A. can be used in a more limited space
    B. measures the torque applied
    C. will not strip the threads of a bolt
    D. is available for all sizes of hex bolts

    3.____

4. The sum of 5 feet 4 1/4 inches, 8 feet 7 1/2 inches, and 13 feet 5 3/4 inches is _____ feet _____ inches.

    A. 26; 6 3/4
    B. 27; 5 1/2
    C. 27; 7 1/2
    D. 28; 8 3/4

    4.____

5. If the floor area of one shop is 17 feet by 19 feet 3 inches and the floor area of an adjacent shop is 22 feet by 28 feet 6 inches, then the TOTAL floor area of these two shops is MOST NEARLY _____ square feet.

    A. 856   B. 946   C. 948   D. 954

    5.____

6. A carton contains 9 dozen drill bits.
    If a helper removes 73 drill bits, the number of bits remaining in the carton is

    A. 27   B. 35   C. 47   D. 62

    6.____

7. The nominal voltage of the *D* size dry-cell battery used in common hand-held flashlights is MOST NEARLY _____ volt(s).

    A. 1   B. 1.5   C. 2.0   D. 2.5

    7.____

8. In an electric circuit, a volt-ohmmeter can be used to DIRECTLY measure

    A. inductance
    B. power
    C. resistance
    D. capacitance

    8.____

9. An ammeter is a device used for measuring the 9.____

   A. current in an electric circuit
   B. dimensions of small mechanical parts
   C. voltage in an electric circuit
   D. depth of holes

10. The purpose of a water trap in a plumbing drainage system is to 10.____

    A. prevent the leakage of water
    B. prevent freezing of the pipes
    C. block off sewer gas
    D. reduce the water pressure in the system

11. Small leaks in a compressed air pipe line leading from a shop compressor are MOST easily located by 11.____

    A. creating a vacuum in the air line
    B. allowing the compressor to pump water through the lines
    C. monitoring air gauges throughout the piping system
    D. applying soapy water to the pipeline

12. A helper is paid at the rate of $5.04 per hour and receives time and one-half for any hours he works over 40 hours. 12.____
    If he works 50 hours during a certain work week, his GROSS earnings should be

    A. $252.00 B. $262.20 C. $277.20 D. $302.40

13. Tubing with an outside diameter of 2" and a wall thickness of 1/16" has an inside diameter which is 13.____

    A. 1 1/2" B. 1 3/4" C. 1 7/8" D. 1 15/16"

14. The tool that holds the die when threading pipe is GENERALLY called a 14.____

    A. vise B. stock C. yoke D. coupling

15. A fitting used to join a small pipe at right angles to the middle of a large pipe is called a 15.____

    A. union   B. coupling
    C. cap   D. reducing tee

16. Gaskets are COMMONLY used between the flanges of large pipe joints to 16.____

    A. make a leakproof connection
    B. provide for expansion
    C. provide space for assembly
    D. adjust for poor alignment

17. The pipe fitting that should be used to connect a 1" pipe to a 1 1/2" valve is called a 17.____

    A. reducing coupling   B. nipple
    C. bushing   D. union

18. To prevent damage to an air compressor, the air coming into the compressor is USUALLY

   A. cooled   B. heated   C. expanded   D. filtered

19. A steel rod having a diameter of 2 1/4 inches is to be discarded when its diameter is worn down more than .075 inches.
    The MINIMUM diameter permissible for this rod is _____ inches.

   A. 1.175   B. 2.000   C. 2.175   D. 2.235

20. The reason for galvanizing sheet metal is to

   A. make it harder
   B. increase its tensile strength
   C. prevent it from being a conductor of electricity
   D. make it rust-resistant

21. A hole drilled in a shaft would PROBABLY be reamed to fit a

   A. lag screw
   B. cap screw
   C. carriage bolt
   D. taper pin

22. The part of a drill press which is used to hold the drill bit is called a

   A. chuck   B. collar   C. bit   D. vise

23. When administering first aid to a helper suffering from shock as a result of falling off a high ladder, it is MOST important to

   A. cover the helper and keep him warm
   B. give the helper something to drink
   C. apply artificial respiration to the helper
   D. prop the helper up to a sitting position

24. Safety shoes usually have the *unique* feature of

   A. extra hard heels and soles to prevent nails from piercing the shoes
   B. special leather to prevent the piercing of the shoes by falling objects
   C. a metal guard over the toes which is built into the shoes
   D. a non-slip tread on the heels and soles

25. If a co-worker's clothing gets caught in the gears of a machine in operation, the FIRST thing for a helper to do is to

   A. call the supervisor
   B. try to pull him out
   C. shut off the machine's power
   D. jam a metal tool between the gears of the machine

26. Of the following, the MOST important factor contributing to a helper's safety on the job is for him to

   A. work slowly
   B. wear gloves
   C. be alert
   D. know his job well

27. If it is necessary for you to lift one end of a piece of heavy equipment with a crow bar in order to allow a maintainer to work underneath it, the BEST of the following procedures to follow is to

    A. support the handle of the bar on a box
    B. insert temporary blocks to support the piece
    C. call the supervisor to help you
    D. wear heavy gloves

28. The part of a bus that allows one rear wheel to turn faster or slower than the other when turning a corner is the

    A. universal joint   B. rear axle
    C. idler   D. differential

29. In a 4-stroke cycle diesel engine, the fuel is ignited by means of

    A. compressed air at a high temperature
    B. special spark plugs
    C. cold spark plugs
    D. hot spark plugs

30. The basic purpose of an idler gear in a gear train is to

    A. change gear speed
    B. increase gear torque
    C. reduce friction in the gear train
    D. change the direction of rotation of a shaft

KEY (CORRECT ANSWERS)

1.	B	16.	A
2.	C	17.	C
3.	A	18.	D
4.	B	19.	C
5.	D	20.	D
6.	B	21.	D
7.	B	22.	A
8.	C	23.	A
9.	A	24.	C
10.	C	25.	C
11.	D	26.	C
12.	C	27.	B
13.	C	28.	D
14.	B	29.	A
15.	D	30.	D

TEST 3

DIRECTIONS: Each question or incomplete statement is followed by several suggested answers or completions. Select the one that BEST answers the question or completes the statement. *PRINT THE LETTER OF THE CORRECT ANSWER IN THE SPACE AT THE RIGHT.*

1. The jaws of a vise close 3/16 inch for each turn of the screw. 1.____
   If the vise is open 3 3/8 inches, then the number of turns needed to close the jaw is

   A. 16　　　　　B. 17　　　　　C. 18　　　　　D. 24

2. When cutting a left-hand thread on a lathe, it is NECESSARY to reverse the direction of the 2.____

   A. chuck　　　　　　　　　B. driving motor
   C. lead screw　　　　　　　D. lathe centers

3. In order to cut a 2-inch diameter hole accurately into a sheet of 16 gauge sheet metal, it is BEST to use a 3.____

   A. cutter and a bar　　　　B. hand reamer
   C. high speed drill　　　　　D. nibbler

4. The instrument that is COMMONLY used to check the armature of small D.C. motors for shorts, grounds or an open circuit is a(n) 4.____

   A. ammeter　　　　　　　　B. dynamometer
   C. growler　　　　　　　　　D. voltmeter

5. In some plant operations, D.C. current is required where only A.C. is supplied. 5.____
   A device that is used to convert the A.C. to D.C. current is called a(n)

   A. inductor coil　　　　　　B. motor-generator
   C. rheostat　　　　　　　　D. transformer

6. Of the following, the MOST important use for a flexible coupling is to connect two shafts which may 6.____

   A. rotate in opposite directions
   B. have different diameters
   C. occasionally become slightly misaligned
   D. rotate at different speeds

7. The PURPOSE of the packing which is generally found in the stuffing box of a centrifugal pump is to 7.____

   A. *prevent* the impeller from chattering
   B. *prevent* the leakage of fluid
   C. *reduce* bearing wear
   D. *reduce* the discharge pressure

8. A bus wheel which is unbalanced should be rebalanced by 8.____

   A. retreading the tire
   B. bending the rim slightly
   C. replacing the wheel bearing
   D. adding weights at the rim

9. *Truing* a grinding wheel refers to

   A. making the face of the wheel parallel to the spindle
   B. centering the wheel mounting hole
   C. making the face of the wheel larger
   D. mounting the wheel onto the spindle

10. If a main gear having 45 teeth is revolving at 360 RPM, then the speed of a 15-tooth pinion driving this gear is _____ RPM.

    A. 120   B. 180   C. 1080   D. 1800

11. A flux is applied during a brazing operation PRIMARILY to

    A. *prevent* fusion and penetration throughout the joint
    B. *prevent* formation of oxide films in the area of the joint
    C. *reduce* the electrical conductivity of the joint
    D. *reduce* the surface hardness in the area of the joint

12. When grinding a flat chisel, it is GOOD practice to keep the chisel moving across the face of the grinding wheel in order to prevent

    A. grooving of the wheel
    B. burning of the chisel tip
    C. the wheel from vibrating
    D. the wheel from cracking

13. If a brake drum measuring 14 9/16" I.D. is remachined to remove 60 thousandths of an inch from the diameter, the NEW diameter will measure MOST NEARLY

    A. 14.502"   B. 14.563"   C. 14.569"   D. 14.623"

14. An electrical ballast is used in a(n)

    A. heavy duty electric power drill
    B. motor-generator set
    C. electrical circuit breaker
    D. fluorescent lighting system

15. An electrical transformer can be used to

    A. raise battery output voltage
    B. maintain constant battery output voltage
    C. lower the voltage from a 110 volt A.C. power line
    D. change the current from A.C. to D.C.

16. Metals are commonly arc-welded electrically by the use of _____ voltage and _____ current.

    A. high; high   B. high; low
    C. low; high   D. low; low

17. A pinion with 21 teeth engages a gear rack having 14 teeth per inch. When the rack has moved 1 inch, the pinion will have rotated through _____ degrees.

    A. 120   B. 180   C. 240   D. 360

Questions 18-22.

DIRECTIONS: Read the information below carefully. Then answer Questions 18 through 22 on the basis of this information.

TITANIC AIR COMPRESSOR

Valves: The compressors are equipped with Titanic plate valves which are automatic in operation. Valves are so constructed that an entire valve assembly can readily be removed from the head. The valves provide large port area with short lift and are accurately guided to insure positive seating.

Starting Unloader: Each compressor (or air end) is equipped with a centrifugal governor which is bolted directed to the compressor crank shaft. The governor actuates cylinder relief valves so as to relieve pressure from the cylinders during starting and stopping. The motor is never required to start the compressor under load.

Air Strainer: Each cylinder air inlet connection is fitted with a suitable combination air strainer and muffler.

Pistons: Pistons are lightweight castings, ribbed internally to secure strength and are accurately turned and ground. Each piston is fitted with four (4) rings, two of which are oil control rings. Piston pins are hardened and tempered steel of the full floating type. Bronze bushings are used between piston pin and piston.

Connecting Rods: Connecting rods are of solid bronze designed for maximum strength, rigidity, and wear. Crank pins are fitted with renewable steel bushings. Connecting rods are of the one-piece type, there being no bolts, nuts, or cotter pins which can come loose. With this type of construction, wear is reduced to a negligible amount, and adjustment of wrist pin and crank pin bearings is unnecessary.

Main Bearings: Main bearings are of the ball type and are securely held in position by spacers. This type of bearing entirely eliminates the necessity of frequent adjustment or attention. The crank shaft is always in perfect alignment.

Crank Shaft: The crank shaft is a one-piece heat-treated forging of best quality open-hearth steel, of rugged design, and of sufficient size to transmit the motor power and any additional stresses which may occur in service. Each crank shaft is counter-balanced (dynamically balanced) to reduce vibration to a minimum, and is accurately machined to properly receive the ball bearing races, crank pin bushing, flexible coupling, and centrifugal governor. Suitable provision is made to insure proper lubrication of all crank shaft bearings and bushings with the minimum amount of attention.

Coupling: Compressor and motor shafts are connected through a Morse Chain Company all-metal enclosed flexible coupling. This coupling consists of two sprockets, one mounted on, and keyed to, each shaft; the sprockets are wrapped by a single Morse Chain, the entire assembly being enclosed in a split aluminum grease packed cover.

18. The crank pin of the connecting rod is fitted with a renewable bushing made of

   A. solid bronze
   B. steel
   C. a slight-weight casting
   D. ball bearings

19. When the connecting rod is of the one-piece type,

   A. the wrist pins require frequent adjustment
   B. the crank pins require frequent adjustment
   C. the cotter pins frequently will come loose
   D. wear is reduced to a negligible amount

20. The centrifugal governor is bolted DIRECTLY to the

   A. compressor crank shaft
   B. main bearing
   C. piston pin
   D. muffler

21. The number of oil control rings required for each piston is

   A. one   B. two   C. three   D. four

22. The compressor and motor shafts are connected through a flexible coupling. These couplings are _____ to the shafts.

   A. keyed
   B. brazed
   C. soldered
   D. press fit

23. Before drilling a hole in a steel plate, an indentation should be made with a

   A. center punch
   B. nail
   C. drill bit
   D. pin punch

24. Of the following, the BEST way to lay out a 30-foot long straight line on a floor is to use

   A. a steel tape and carpenter's pencil
   B. chalk and a 6-foot rule
   C. chalk and a plumb bob
   D. chalk and a mason's line

25. Air supply reservoirs are generally equipped with relief valves. The PURPOSE of these valves is to

   A. compensate for air leakage from the reservoir
   B. drain water caused by condensation
   C. protect the reservoir against excessive air pressure
   D. disconnect the air supply reservoir from the supply line

KEY (CORRECT ANSWERS)

1. C
2. C
3. A
4. C
5. B

6. C
7. B
8. D
9. A
10. C

11. B
12. A
13. D
14. D
15. C

16. C
17. C
18. B
19. D
20. A

21. B
22. A
23. A
24. D
25. C

———

MECHANICAL APTITUDE
TOOLS AND THEIR USE
EXAMINATION SECTION
TEST 1

DIRECTIONS: Each question or incomplete statement is followed by several suggested answers or completions. Select the one that BEST answers the question or completes the statement. *PRINT THE LETTER OF THE CORRECT ANSWER IN THE SPACE AT THE RIGHT.*

Questions 1-15.

DIRECTIONS: Questions 1 through 15 refer to the tools shown below. The numbers in the answers refer to the numbers beneath the tools. NOTE: These tools are NOT shown to scale.

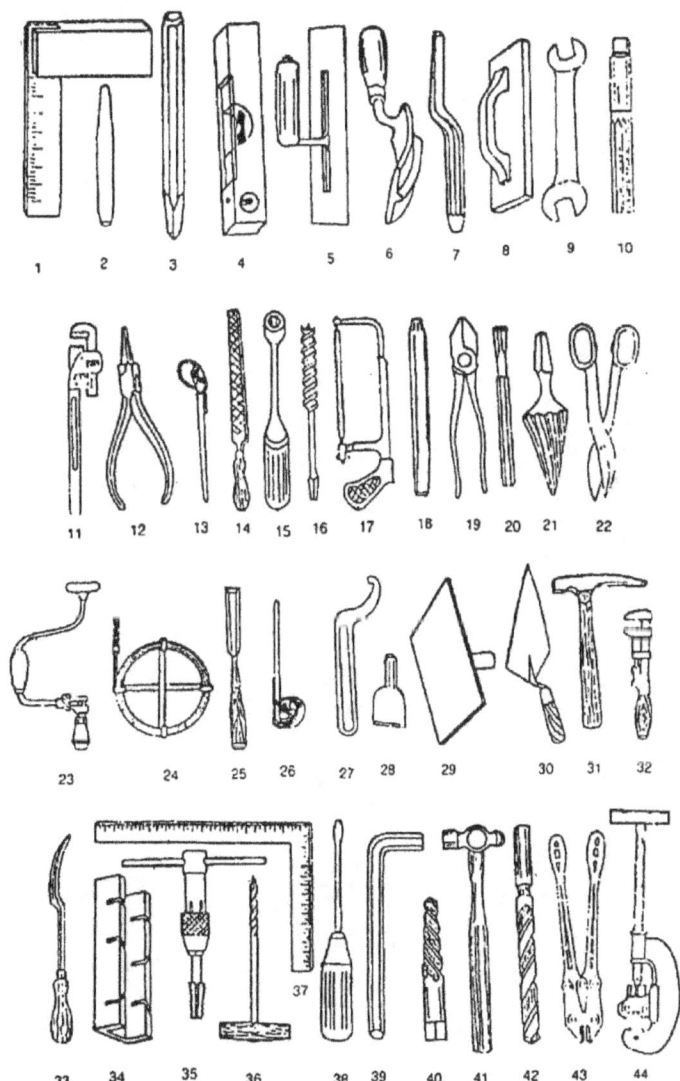

2 (#1)

1. A "pipe reamer" is tool number
   A. 2   B. 10   C. 21   D. 24   1.____

2. A "mitre box" is tool number
   A. 1   B. 4   C. 25   D. 34   2.____

3. A "bolt cutter" is tool number
   A. 3   B. 25   C. 40   D. 43   3.____

4. The proper "drill bit" for wood is tool number
   A. 10   B. 16   C. 21   D. 40   4.____

5. A "ball peen" is tool number
   A. 20   B. 31   C. 33   D. 41   5.____

6. A "hawk" is tool number
   A. 5   B. 28   C. 29   D. 30   6.____

7. "Snips" is tool number
   A. 12   B. 19   C. 22   D. 43   7.____

8. A "bull point" is tool number
   A. 3   B. 7   C. 10   D. 20   8.____

9. An "open-end wrench" is tool number
   A. 9   B. 11   C. 15   D. 27   9.____

10. A "drift pin" is tool number
   A. 2   B. 3   C. 10   D. 40   10.____

11. A "pipe cutter" is tool number
   A. 17   B. 18   C. 28   D. 44   11.____

12. A "trowel" is tool number
   A. 6   B. 8   C. 28   D. 30   12.____

13. A "square" is tool number
   A. 4   B. 29   C. 34   D. 37   13.____

14. A "float" is tool number
   A. 8   B. 28   C. 29   D. 30   14.____

15. A "snake" is tool number
   A. 13   B. 24   C. 26   D. 36   15.____

KEY (CORRECT ANSWERS)

1.	C	6.	C	11.	D
2.	D	7.	C	12.	D
3.	D	8.	A	13.	D
4.	B	9.	A	14.	A
5.	D	10.	A	15.	B

TEST 2

DIRECTIONS: Each question or incomplete statement is followed by several suggested answers or completions. Select the one that BEST answers the question or completes the statement. *PRINT THE LETTER OF THE CORRECT ANSWER IN THE SPACE AT THE RIGHT.*

1. The tool shown at the right is a
   A. countersink
   B. counterbore
   C. star drill
   D. burring reamer

   1.____

2. The saw shown at the right would be used to cut
   A. curved designs in thin wood
   B. strap iron
   C. asphalt tiles to fit against walls
   D. soft lead pipe

   2.____

3. The tool shown at the right is a
   A. float
   B. finishing trowel
   C. hawk
   D. roofing seamer

   3.____

4. The hammer shown to the right would be used by a
   A. carpenter
   B. bricklayer
   C. tinsmith
   D. plumber

   4.____

5. When drilling into a steel plate, the MOST likely cause for the breaking of a drill bit is
   A. too low a drill speed
   B. excessive cutting oil lubricant
   C. too much drill pressure
   D. using a bit with a dull point

   5.____

6. Of the following, the MOST important advantage of a ratchet wrench over an open-end wrench is that the ratchet wrench
   A. can be used in a more limited space
   B. measures the torque applied
   C. will not strip the threads of a bolt
   D. is available for all sizes of hex bolts

   6.____

7. The tool that holds the die when threading pipe is generally called a
   A. vise   B. stock   C. yoke   D. coupling

   7.____

8. A fitting used to join a small pipe at right angles to the middle of a large pie is called a
   A. union   B. coupling   C. cap   D. reducing tee

9. Gaskets are commonly used between the flanges of large pipe joints to
   A. make a leakproof connection   B. provide for expansion
   C. provide space for assembly   D. adjust for poor alignment

10. The pipe fitting that should be used to connect a 1" pipe to a 1½" valve is called a
    A. reducing coupling   B. nipple
    C. bushing   D. union

11. The part of a drill press which is used to hold the drill bit is called a
    A. chuck   B. collar   C. bit   D. vise

12. When grinding a flat chisel, it is GOOD practice to keep the chisel moving across the face of the grinding wheel in order to prevent
    A. grooving of the wheel   B. burning of the chisel tip
    C. the wheel from vibrating D. the wheel from cracking

13. In order to determine if a surface is *truly* horizontal, it should be checked with a
    A. carpenters square   B. plumb bob
    C. steel rule   D. spirit level

14. A gauge of a nail indicates the
    A. length of the shank   B. diameter of the head
    C. thickness of the head   D. diameter of the shank

15. A tool can be used BOTH for scribing regular arcs and also for transferring dimensions is the
    A. trammel   B. protractor
    C. scriber   D. combination square

16. The devices for clamping sheet metal in place on a squaring shear are the
    A. clamps   B. hold-downs   C. guides   D. square

17. When a hacksaw is used to cut out sheet metal, the BEST blade to use is one with _____ teeth per inch.
    A. 14   B. 18   C. 24   D. 32

18. A tool which may be attached to a drill press and used to cut circles of 2½" diameter or larger in sheet metal is the
    A. twist drill   B. circular saw   C. reamer   D. hole saw

19. A versatile hand tool that can be used for a variety of sheet metalwork jobs such as bucking up rivet heads, straightening kinks in formed metal, forming seals, etc. is the
    A. hand dolly
    B. universal iron worker
    C. cupping tool
    D. set hammer

20. To make certain two points separated by a vertical distance of 8 feet are in perfect vertical alignment, it would be BEST to use a(n)
    A. surface gage
    B. height gage
    C. protractor
    D. plumb bob

21. A claw hammer is PROPERLY used for
    A. driving a cold chisel
    B. driving brads
    C. setting rivets
    D. flattening a ½" metal bar

22. It would NOT be good practice to tighten a 1" hexagon nut with a(n) _____ wrench.
    A. monkey
    B. 1" fixed open-end
    C. adjustable open-end
    D. stillson

23. Lock washers are used PRINCIPALLY with _____ screws.
    A. machine   B. wood   C. self-tapping   D. lag

24. Toggle bolts are MOST appropriate for use to fasten conduit clamps to a
    A. steel column
    B. concrete wall
    C. hollow tile wall
    D. brick wall

25. If a 10-24 by ¾" machine screw is not available, the screw which could be MOST easily modified to use in an emergency is a
    A. 10-24 by ½"
    B. 12-24 by ¾"
    C. 10-2 by 1½"
    D. 8-24 by ¾"

26. Of the following tools, the one that should be used to cut thin-wall metal tubing is the
    A. reamer   B. plier   C. hacksaw   D. broach

27. A wrench that can be used to tighten a nut to a specified tightness is a _____ wrench.
    A. bonney   B. spud   C. torque   D. adjustable

28. The one of the following that will MOST likely show a "mushroomed" head is a
    A. cold chisel
    B. file cleaner
    C. screwdriver blade
    D. ratchet

29. A tool that is used to bend pipe is the
    A. lintel   B. hickey   C. collet   D. brace

30. Before drilling a hole in a steel plate, an indentation should be made with a   30.____
    A. center punch   B. nail   C. drill bit   D. pin punch

KEY (CORRECT ANSWERS)

1.	D	11.	A	21.	B
2.	A	12.	A	22.	D
3.	A	13.	D	23.	A
4.	B	14.	D	24.	C
5.	C	15.	A	25.	C
6.	A	16.	B	26.	C
7.	B	17.	D	27.	C
8.	D	18.	D	28.	A
9.	A	19.	A	29.	B
10.	C	20.	D	30.	A

ARITHMETICAL REASONING

EXAMINATION SECTION

TEST 1

DIRECTIONS: Each question or incomplete statement is followed by several suggested answers or completions. Select the one that BEST answers the question or completes the statement. *PRINT THE LETTER OF THE CORRECT ANSWER IN THE SPACE AT THE RIGHT.*

1. The sum of the fractions 3/32, 3/16, 3/8, and 3/4 is equal to 1.____
   A. 1 13/32 B. 1 5/16 C. 1 7/8 D. 3

2. If a maintainer earns $11.52 per hour, and time and one-half for overtime, his gross salary for a week in which he works 5 hours over his regular 40 hours should be 2.____
   A. $460.80 B. $518.80 C. $547.20 D. $578.80

3. If the diameter of a shaft must be 2.620 inches plus or minus .002 inches, the shaft will be SATISFACTORY if it has a diameter of _____ inches. 3.____
   A. 2.518 B. 2.600 C. 2.617 D. 2.621

4. A bus part costs $275 per 100 when purchased from a vendor. The bus part could be made in the bus machine shop at a labor cost of $60 for 50 units, with material and other costs amounting to $25 for 25 units.
   If 100 such parts were made in the bus shop, there would be a saving of 4.____
   A. $55 B. $95 C. $140 D. $165

5. The sum of 9/16", 11/32", 15/64", and 1 3/32" is MOST NEARLY 5.____
   A. 2.234" B. 2.134" C. 2.334" D. 2.214"

6. The diameter of a circle whose circumference is 14.5" is MOST NEARLY 6.____
   A. 4.62" B. 4.81" C. 4.72" D. 4.51"

7. A bus part cost $90 per 100 when purchased from a vendor. The bus part could be made in the bus machine shop at a labor cost of $20 for 50 units and material and other costs amounting to $10 for 25 units.
   If 100 such parts are made in the bus stop, there would be a saving of 7.____
   A. $10 B. $30 C. $40 D. $60

8. A bus storage battery having a 300 ampere-hour capacity is 50% discharged. If the bus running schedule for the day is such that the battery will be charging at an average rate of 30 amperes for 2½ hours and discharging at an average rate of 9 amperes for 5 hours, then at the end of the day, the battery will be APPROXIMATELY 8.____
   A. at full charge
   B. 75% charged
   C. 60% charged
   D. 50% charged

9. If the total time allowance for replacing the glass in a broken bus window is 75 minutes, how many jobs of this kind would a maintainer be expected to do in 40 hours of work?
   A. 32　　　B. 40　　　C. 60　　　D. 72

10. A certain rod is tapered so that it changes diameter at a rate of ¼ inch per foot of length.
    If the tapered rod is 3 inches long, then the difference in diameter between the two ends is MOST NEARLY
    A. 0.250"　　　B. 0.187"　　　C. 0.135"　　　D. 0.062"

11. How many 9½ inch long pieces of copper tubing can be cut from a 20-foot length of tubing?
    A. 24　　　B. 25　　　C. 26　　　D. 27

12. Two splice plates must be cut from a piece of sheet steel that has an overall length of 14 3/8 inches. The plates are to be 7 5/8 inches and 5 1/4 inches long. If $1/16$ inch is allowed for each saw cut, then how much material would be left?
    A. 1 3/8"　　　B. 1 1/2"　　　C. 1 5/8"　　　D. 1 3/4"

13. A maintainer requires several lengths of tubing for oil lines as follows: $12^{7}/_{16}$ inches, 5/16 inches, 9 3/16 inches, 9 1/8 inches, 6 1/4 inches, and 5 inches. The TOTAL length of tubing required is MOST NEARLY _____ feet.
    A. 2　　　B. 3　　　C. 4　　　D. 5

14. Two-thirds of 10 feet is MOST NEARLY
    A. 6'2"　　　B. 6'8"　　　C. 6'11"　　　D. 7'1"

15. You are directed to pick up a tray load of brake shoes. The combined weight of tray and brake shoes is 4,000 pounds. Assume that each brake shoe weighs 40 pounds and the tray weighs 240 pounds.
    The number of brake shoes in the tray is MOST NEARLY
    A. 88　　　B. 94　　　C. 100　　　D. 106

16. A maintainer earns $37.32 per hour, and time and one-half for overtime over 40 hours. Each week, 15 percent of his total salary is deducted for social security and taxes. Also, each week a $54.00 deduction is made for a savings bond and a $27.00 deduction is made for a charitable organization.
    If he works a total of 46 hours in a week, his take-home pay for that week is
    A. $1,828.50　　　B. $1,554.30　　　C. $1,473.38　　　D. $1,232.10

17. A rectangularly-shaped repair facility for light trucks is 160 feet wide and 260 feet long. A 10-foot space is provided along each wall for benches and equipment. A 60-foot wide area in the middle of the floor is to remain clear for its entire 260 foot length. The entrance to the shop is at one end of this open area.
    Assuming that there are no columns to contend with, the MAXIMUM area available for parking of trucks is _____ sq. ft.
    A. 15,600　　　B. 19,200　　　C. 26,000　　　D. 41,600

18. A criterion is established that limits the yearly major repair expenses to 30% of the current value of the equipment. Equipment is depreciated at a rate of 20% of its original cost each year. A truck purchased on January 1, 2017 for $27,000 had a reconditioned engine installed in February 2020 at a total cost of $2,700. The amount of money available for additional major repairs on this truck in 2020 is
    A. none   B. $540   C. $1,080   D. $2,160

18.____

19. Twenty carburetors are ordered for your shop by the Purchasing Department. The terms are list, less 30% less 10%, less 5%.
    If the list price of a carburetor is $210 and all terms are met upon delivery, the charges to your budget will be
    A. $4,078.80   B. $3,256.20   C. $2,513.70   D. $1,892.40

19.____

20. The sum of the fractions 7/16", 11/16", 5/32", and 7/8" is MOST NEARLY
    A. 2.1753"   B. 2.1563"   C. 1.9522"   D. 1.9463"

20.____

21. If 750 feet of wire weighs 60 lbs., the number of pounds that 150 feet will weigh is MOST NEARLY
    A. 12   B. 10   C. 8   D. 6

21.____

22. A steel rod 19.750" long is to have three pieces cut from its length. One piece is to be 3.250" long, the second 6.500" long, and the third piece 5.375".
    If .125" is allowed for each cut, the length of the material left over is
    A. 3.750"   B. 4.250"   C. 4.500"   D. 5.150"

22.____

23. If the distance between the north and south terminals is 10.8 miles and a train makes six roundtrips, then the total mileage would be NEAREST _____ miles.
    A. 22   B. 65   C. 130   D. 145

23.____

24. If the thickness of material worn from a car wheel is approximately 1/16 inch off the diameter in 20,000 miles of travel, the wheel diameter will be reduced from 33 inches to 32 3/4 inches after _____ miles.
    A. 60,000   B. 80,000   C. 100,000   D. 120,000

24.____

25. If the distance between north and south terminals is 11.3 miles and a train makes five roundtrips, then the total travel mileage would be NEAREST _____ miles.
    A. 23   B. 55   C. 115   D. 130

25.____

KEY (CORRECT ANSWERS)

1.	A		11.	B
2.	C		12.	A
3.	D		13.	D
4.	A		14.	B
5.	A		15.	B
6.	A		16.	C
7.	A		17.	B
8.	C		18.	B
9.	A		19.	C
10.	D		20.	B

21. A
22. B
23. C
24. B
25. C

SOLUTIONS TO PROBLEMS

1. $\frac{3}{32} + \frac{3}{16} + \frac{3}{8} + \frac{3}{4} = \frac{45}{32} = 1\frac{13}{32}$

2. Gross salary = ($11.52)(40) + ($17.28)(5) = $547.20

3. 2.620 ± .002 means from 2.618 to 2.622. The only selection in this range is 2.621.

4. ($60)($\frac{100}{50}$) + ($25)($\frac{100}{25}$)$220 if made in the bus shop. Savings = $275 - $220 = $55

5. 9/16" + 11/32" + 15/64" + 1 3/32" = 143/64 = 2 15/64" = 2.234"

6. Diameter = 14.5" ÷ π ≈ 4.62"

7. ($20)($\frac{100}{50}$) + ($10)($\frac{100}{25}$) = $80 if made in the bus shop. Savings = $990 - $80 = $10

8. [150+[(30(2 1/2)] − [(9)(5)] = [150+75] − 45 = 180, and 180/300 = 60%

9. (40)(60) ÷ 75 = 32

10. (1/4")(3/12) = 1/16" ≈ .062"

11. (20)(12) = 240", and 240" ÷ 9 1/2" ≈ 25.3 rounded down to 25 pieces of tubing

12. 14 3/8" − 7 5/8" − 5 1/4" − 1/16" = 1 3/8"

13. 12 7/16" + 14 5/16" + 9 3/16" + 9 1/8" + 6 1/4" + 5" ≈ 5 ft.

14. (2/3)(10') = 6 2/3' = 6'8"

15. 4000 − 240 = 3760 lbs. Then, 3760 ÷ 40 = 94 brake shoes

16. Take-home pay = ($37.32)(40) + ($55.98)(6) − .15[($37.32)(40) + ($55.98)(6)] - $54.00 - $27.00 = $1,473.738 ≈ $1,473.38

17. Subtracting the area for benches and equipment would leave an area of 240' by 140'. Now, deduct the 60' width. Final area = (240')(80') = 19,200 sq.ft.

18. In 2020, the value of the truck = $27,000 − (3)(.20)($27,000) = $10,800. The limit of the expenses for repairs = (.30)($10,800) = $3,240. After installing engine, $3,240 - $2,700 = $540 left for additional major repairs.

19. (20)($210)(.70)(.90)(.95) = $2,513.70

20. 7/16" + 11/16" + 5/32" + 7/8" = 69/32" ≈ 2.1563"

6 (#1)

21. (150/750)(60) = 12 lbs.

22. 19.750" − 3.250" − 6.500" − 5.375" − .125" − .125" − 1.25" = 4.250" left over

23. (6)(10.8)(2) = 129.6 ≈ 130 miles

24. 33" − 32 3/4" = 1/4". Then, (1/4 ÷ 1/16)(20,000) = 80,000 miles

25. (5)(11.3)(2) = 113 miles, closest to 115 miles

TEST 2

DIRECTIONS: Each question or incomplete statement is followed by several suggested answers or completions. Select the one that BEST answers the question or completes the statement. *PRINT THE LETTER OF THE CORRECT ANSWER IN THE SPACE AT THE RIGHT.*

1. In looking over an alteration job on car bodies, you find that 96 pieces of 1" × 1" × 1'6" long square steel stock are needed to do this job. Steel weighs 480 lbs. per cu. ft. and costs $0.12 per lb.
   The total cost of this material is MOST NEARLY
   A. $40.00   B. $60.00   C. $80.00   D. $100.00   1.____

2. Assume that the breakdown cost of a particular motor job is as follows:
   Parts $160.00
   Labor   75.00
   Overhead   30.00
   The percentage of the total cost for labor is MOST NEARLY
   A. 20%   B. 25%   C. 28%   D. 32%   2.____

3. The engine hydraulic system and transmission on a certain type of tractor use the same type oil. This oil is delivered in 55 gallon drums.
   How many drums are needed to make all three changes on 10 of these tractors whose capacities are the following:
   Engine   58 quarts
   Transmission   70 quarts
   Hydraulic system   22 gallons
   A. 100   B. 50   C. 54   D. 10   3.____

4. A new shop layout requires the following:
   1,000 sq. ft. for tool room
   3,000 sq. ft. for parts room
   10,000 sq. ft. for service bays
   5,500 sq. ft. for isles
   The building should be AT LEAST _____ yards wide and 70 yards long.
   A. 10   B. 20   C. 25   D. 30   4.____

5. When filling a diesel engine cooling system, the mix required is 80% antifreeze and 20% water. You are required to fill seven systems containing 30 gallons each. The number of 5 gallon cans of antifreeze that are required is MOST NEARLY
   A. 210   B. 168   C. 34   D. 26   5.____

6. The floors of 2 cars are to be painted with a special test paint. Assume that the floor area in each car is 600 square feet. A gallon of this paint will cover 400 square feet.
   The number of gallons of this paint that you should pick up at the storeroom to paint the two car floors would be
   A. 6   B. 5   C. 4   D. 3   6.____

7. Assume that you are sent to the storeroom for 1,000 of 600-volt contact tips which are to be distributed equally to 5 foremen, but you find that the storeroom can only supply you with 825.
If you distribute these 825 tips equally to the 5 foremen the number of tips that each foreman will receive is
A. 165   B. 175   C. 190   D. 200

8. You are asked to fill six 5-gallon cans of oil from a full drum containing 52 gallons. When you have filled the six cans, the number of gallons of oil left in the drum will be MOST NEARLY
A. 14   B. 16   C. 22   D. 30

9. A certain wire rope is made up of 6 strands, each strand containing 19 wires. The TOTAL number of wires in this wire rope is
A. 25   B. 96   C. 114   D. 144

10. The hook should be the weakest part of any crane, hoist, or sling.
According to this statement, if a particular hook has a rated capacity of 2½ tons, then the MAXIMUM load that should be lifted with this hook is _____ pounds.
A. 150   B. 3,000   C. 5,000   D. 5,500

11. Assume that 2 car wheels weigh 635 pounds each and are attached to an axle weighing 1,260 pounds.
The total weight of this assembly is MOST NEARLY _____ pounds.
A. 1,270   B. 1,520   C. 1,895   D. 2,530

12. If an employee authorizes his employer to deduct 4% of his $1,200 weekly salary for a savings bond, the MINIMUM number of weekly deductions required to get enough money to buy a bond costing $144 is
A. 3   B. 6   C. 8   D. 9

13. In weighing out a truckful of scrap metal, the scale reads 21,496 lbs.
If the empty truck weighs 9,879 lbs., the amount of scrap metal, in pounds, is MOST NEARLY
A. 10,507   B. 10,602   C. 11,617   D. 12,617

14. Four trays of material are placed on the body of a delivery truck for delivery to the inspection shop. Each tray is 4 feet wide and 4 feet long.
If these trays are placed side by side on the floor of the delivery truck, together they will cover an area of the floor MOST NEARLY _____ square feet.
A. 32   B. 48   C. 64   D. 72

15. Assume that you are operating a degreasing tank and its tray holds 5 gear cases.
It takes 40 minutes to clean one tray of gear cases.
At the end of 6 hours of operation (excluding lunch break and loading and unloading time), the number of gear case cleaned will be
A. 30   B. 36   C. 45   D. 50

3 (#2)

16. If a serviceman's weekly gross salary is $160 and 20% is deducted for taxes, his take-home pay is
    A. $120   B. $128   C. $140   D. $144

Questions 17-18.

DIRECTIONS: Questions 17 and 18 are to be answered on the basis of the following paragraph.

The car maintenance department is considering the purchase of a certain car part from Manufacturer X for $140. An equivalent part can be purchased from Manufacturer Y for $100. The part made by Manufacturer X must be reconditioned every 3 years, using material costing $30 and requiring 6 hours of labor. The part made by Manufacturer Y must be reconditioned every 1½ years, using material costing $24 and requiring 5 hours of labor. The maintainer's rate of pay is $12 per hour.

17. The cost of operating with the part made by Manufacturer X (excluding the first cost) is MOST NEARLY _____ per year.
    A. $30   B. $32   C. $34   D. $42

18. The total cost of operating with the part made by Manufacturer Y over a period of 12 years, including the first cost of the part and assuming the part is scrapped at the end of 12 years, is MOST NEARLY
    A. $472   B. $572   C. $688   D. $772

19. The area of the steel plate shown in the sketch at the right is _____ sq. ft.
    A. 16
    B. 18
    C. 20
    D. 22

20. A car part made by a Manufacturer X has a purchase cost of $7,500 and a life of 5 years. It requires a yearly maintenance cost of $50. Manufacturer Y offers a similar part of this type for $4,800, with a life of 3 years and a yearly maintenance cost of $75.
    By purchasing the part offering a better overall value, the yearly savings per unit purchased would be
    A. $115   B. $125   C. $135   D. $140

21. A car part can be overhauled at the rate of 12 parts per hour. Each part requires new material costing $6 each.
    If the labor cost is $14 per hour, one part can be overhauled for a total cost (labor plus material) of MOST NEARLY
    A. $6.64   B. $7.16   C. $7.46   D. $8.20

4 (#2)

22. A car part costs $150 per 50 units when purchased in a finished condition from a vendor. The car part can be made in the shop at a total cost off $2.20 per unit, when made on a machine which can be purchased for $1,000.
The MINIMUM number of parts which must be made on this machine before the savings equal the cost of the machine is
A. 850 B. 1,000 C. 1,250 D. 1,500

23. A pound of a certain type of metal washer contains 360 washers.
If ¼ of the material of each washer is removed by enlarging the center of each washer, the number of washers to the pound should then be MOST NEARLY
A. 280 B. 300 C. 380 D. 480

24. A maintainer earns $32.52 per hour, and time and one-half for overtime. Ten percent of his total salary earned is deducted from his paycheck for social security and taxes. He also contributes $15.00 per week to a charitable organization. No other deductions are made.
If he works 2 hours over his basic 40 hours, his weekly take-home pay should be MOST NEARLY
A. $1,398.36 B. $1,258.50 C. $1,243.50 D. $1,231.80

25. A car part costs $130 per 100 units if purchased from a vendor. The car part can be made on a machine which can be purchased for $1,000. Assume that this machine has a production life of 20,000 units with no salvage value, and that all shop costs amount to $80 per 100 units turned out in the shop.
The money that would be SAVED during the life of the machine would be
A. $800 B. $8,000 C. 9,000 D. $18,000

KEY (CORRECT ANSWERS)

1.	B		11.	D
2.	C		12.	A
3.	D		13.	C
4.	D		14.	C
5.	C		15.	C
6.	D		16.	B
7.	A		17.	C
8.	C		18.	C
9.	C		19.	C
10.	C		20.	B

21. B
22. C
23. D
24. C
25. C

SOLUTIONS TO PROBLEMS

1. Total cost ≈ (96)(.01)(4)(.12) ≈ $55, which is closest to $60. Note that 1" × 1" × 1'6" ≈ (1/12')(1/12')(3/2') − 1.96 ≈ .01 cu. ft.

2. Labor = $75 ÷ $265 ≈ 28%

3. (10)(14.5+17.5+22) = 540. Then, 540 ÷ 55 ≈ 10 drums

4. Total sq. ft. = 19,500, which is 2166 2/3 sq. yds. Then, 2166 2/3 ÷ 70 ≈ 30.95 or 31

5. Amount of antifreeze = (.80)(7)(.30) = 168 gallons. Then, 168 ÷ 5 ≈ 34 cans

6. (600+600) ÷ 400 = 3 gallons

7. 825 ÷ 5 = 165 for each foreman

8. 52 − (6)(5) = 22 gallons left

9. (19)(6) = 114 wires

10. (2½)(2000) = 5000 pounds

11. (2)(635) + 1260 = 2530 pounds

12. ($1,200)(.04) = $48. Then, $144 ÷ $48 = 3 weekly deductions

13. 21,496 − 9,879 = 11,617 pounds

14. 4(4')(4') = 64 sq. ft.

15. 6 hrs. ÷ 2/3 hr. = 9 trays = 45 gear cases cleaned

16. Take-home pay = ($160)(.80) = $128

17. ($30)+(6)($12) = ($102 for 3 yrs. = $34 per year

18. 100 + 7(24) + 7(60) = 688

19. Separate the figure into regions as follows:
    I: 1'×2' = 2 sq.ft.
    II: 3'×4' = 12 sq.ft.
    III: (3'×4') ÷ 2 = 6 sq.ft.
    Total = 20 sq.ft.

    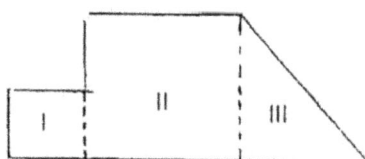

20. Manufacturer X: $7500 + ($50)(5) = $7750, so the cost per year is $7750 ÷ 5 = $1550
    Manufacturer Y: $4800 + (3)($75) = $5025, so the cost per year is $5025 ÷ 3 = $1675
    Using Manufacturer X, savings = $125 per year

21. Cost of 12 parts = (12)($6) + $14 = $86. Then, the cost of one part = $86 ÷ 12 ≈ $7.16.2021

22. Savings per unit is $150/50 - $2.20 = $.80. Then, $1000 ÷ $.80 = 1250

23. 1 – ¼ = ¾. Then, 360 ÷ 34 = 480

24. Take-home pay = [($32.52)(40)+($48.78)(2)][.90] - $15 ≈ $1,243.50

25. Amount if purchased from a vendor = $130(200) = $26,000. Using the machine, amount = $1000 + ($80)(200) = $17,000. Amount saved = $9000

TEST 3

DIRECTIONS: Each question or incomplete statement is followed by several suggested answers or completions. Select the one that BEST answers the question or completes the statement. *PRINT THE LETTER OF THE CORRECT ANSWER IN THE SPACE AT THE RIGHT.*

1. A Cat 983 Traxcavator can make a complete loading cycle from bank to truck and back to bank in 25 seconds.
   If the bucket contains 4 cu. yds of loose material, the MINIMUM amount of material that an operator should load in 4 hours is _____ cubic yards.
   A. 2,304 B. 2,100 C. 1,896 D. 576

   1._____

2. An excavation is 12' × 18' × 15' and is to be dug by a Cat 983 Traxcavator with 3 cubic yards of solid material excavated per pass.
   The MINIMUM number of passes required to dig the hole is _____ passes.
   A. 40 B. 46 C. 120 D. 126

   2._____

3. A Cat D8 tractor and 463 scraper can haul 22 cubic yards of cover material per trip.
   If it is required to cover an area 1,000 feet by 100 feet to a depth of 2 feet, the MINIMUM number of trips that will be required is MOST NEARLY
   A. 284 B. 337 C. 385 D. 421

   3._____

4. Gravel weighs 2,800 pounds per cubic yard.
   In order to carry 42,000 pounds of gravel, the capacity of a truck must be AT LEAST _____ cubic yards.
   A. 10 B. 12 C. 15 D. 18

   4._____

5. The average capacity of an Athey Wagon is 60 cubic yards. The Cat D8 tractor pulls 2 wagons.
   The MINIMUM number of trips to the fill that would be required to empty a barge loaded with 1,000 cubic yards of refuse is
   A. 9 B. 17 C. 30 D. 90

   5._____

6. When pulling 2 Athey trailers, the operator of a Cat D8 tractor can make a round trip from the crane to the fill and back in 15 minutes.
   Assuming that delays and breaks allow the man to work productively for 75% of the shift, the MAXIMUM number of trips that the operator can make in an 8-hour shift is
   A. 43 B. 32 C. 24 D. 16

   6._____

7. In plowing a street which is 24 feet wide, a motor grader can make an 8-ft. wide pass, with a 2-ft. overlap.
   If a roundtrip takes 4 minutes, the MINIMUM time needed to plow this street should be _____ minutes.
   A. 12 B. 16 C. 24 D. 32

   7._____

2 (#3)

8. A scraper is loaded with 23 cubic yards of sand weighing 100 pounds per cubic foot.
   The weight of the load, in tons, is MOST NEARLY
   A. 20   B. 30   C. 40   D. 60

   8.____

9. Assume a crankcase oil change of 6 quarts for every 150 service hours.
   How many 42 gallon drums of oil are required for 8,400 total service hours.
   A. 5   B. 2   C. 1   D. 1 1/3

   9.____

10. Assume that a ruler is marked in 10ths of a foot instead of in inches.
    5 tenths on this ruler would be
    A. 4"   B. 5"   C. 6"   D. 7"

    10.____

11. A truckload of 1½" stone from a 10 cubic yard truck will spread an area APPROXIMATELY _____ long, 6" deep, and _____ wide.
    A. 50'; 10'   B. 10'; 5'   C. 54'; 10'   D. 45'; 5'

    11.____

12. A dump truck with a body 10 ft. long, 5 ft. wide, and 4 ft. deep has a volume of _____ cubic feet.
    A. 150   B. 200   C. 250   D. 300

    12.____

13. A tractor is operated on a given landfill operation during the following time intervals in one day: from 8:15 A.M. to 11:45 A.M.; from 12:30 P.M. to 6:00 P.M.; from 6:45 P.M. to 11:30 P.M.
    The total net operating time, expressed in hours and minutes, is MOST NEARLY
    A. 13; 30   B. 13; 15   C. 13; 45   D. 12; 45

    13.____

14. The area of ground contact (with standard track shoes) of a late model D8 Caterpillar Tractor is 4,296 sq. in.
    Expressed in square feet, this is MOST NEARLY
    A. 358   B. 29.8   C. 159.3   D. 21.37

    14.____

15. A towing winch develops a bare drum line pull of 11.8 tons.
    This force represents, in pounds,
    A. 23,850   B. 28,300   C. 23,800   D. 23,600

    15.____

16. The fuel tank gauge reads about ¾ of a full tank.
    If the tank capacity is 72.5 gallons, the amount of fuel in the tank is MOST NEARLY
    A. 53.2   B. 53.8   C. 54.5   D. 55.0

    16.____

17. If a dump truck capable of carrying 40 2/3 cubic yards is ¾ loaded, it is carrying, in cubic yards,
    A. 28   B. 36½   C. 30½   D. 28 2/3

    17.____

18. A load of sand filling a truck body 6 feet long, 5 feet wide, and 3 feet deep would contain _____ cubic feet.
    A. 14   B. 90   C. 33   D. 21

    18.____

Questions 19-21.

DIRECTIONS: Questions 19 through 21 are to be answered on the basis of the diagrams of balanced levers shown below. P is the center of rotation, W is the weight on the lever, and F is the balancing force.

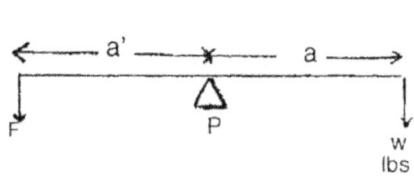
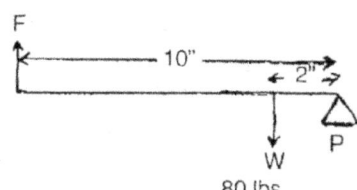

19. In Diagram 1, the force F required to balance the weight W lbs. on the lever shown is equal to _____ lbs.
    A. a/W   B. W/a   C. W   D. Wa

20. In Diagram 2, the force F required to balance the weight of 80 lbs. on the lever shown is _____ lbs.
    A. 4   B. 3   C. 16   D. 32

21. The mechanical advantage of the lever shown in Diagram 2 is
    A. 4   B. 5   C. 8   D. 12

22. The specific gravity of a liquid may be defined as the ratio of the weight of a given volume of the liquid to the weight of an equal volume of water. An empty bottle weighs 5 oz. When the bottle is filled with water, the total weight is 50 oz. When the bottle is filled with another liquid, the total weight is 95 oz. The specific gravity of the second liquid is MOST NEARLY
    A. .50   B. .58   C. 1.7   D. 2.0

23. If one inch is approximately equal to 2.54 centimeters, the number of inches in one meter is MOST NEARLY
    A. 14.2   B. 25.4   C. 39.4   D. 91.4

24. One-quarter divided by five-eighths is
    A. 5/32   B. 1/10   C. 2/5   D. 5/2

25. A man works on a certain job continuously, with no time off for lunch. If he works from 9:45 A.M. until 1:35 P.M. to finish the job, the total time which he spent on the job is MOST NEARLY _____ hours, _____ minutes.
    A. 3; 10   B. 3; 35   C. 3; 50   D. 4; 15

KEY (CORRECT ANSWERS)

1.	A		11.	C
2.	A		12.	B
3.	B		13.	C
4.	C		14.	B
5.	A		15.	D
6.	C		16.	C
7.	B		17.	C
8.	B		18.	B
9.	B		19.	C
10.	C		20.	C

21. B
22. D
23. C
24. C
25. C

SOLUTIONS TO PROBLEMS

1. 4 hrs. = (4)(60)(60) = 14,400 sec. Then, 14,400 ÷ 25 = 576. Thus, (576)(4 cu.yds.) = 2304

2. (12')(18')(15') = 3240 cu.ft. = 120 cu.yds. Then, 120 ÷ 3 = 40

3. (1000')(100')(2') = 200,000 cu.ft. ≈ 7407.4 cu.yds. Finally, 7407.4 ÷ 22 = 336.7, rounded up to 337 trips

4. 42,000 ÷ 2800 = 15 cu.yds.

5. (2)(60 cu.yds.) = 120 yds. Then, 1000 ÷ 120 = 8 1/3, which must be rounded up to 9 trips.

6. 8 hrs. ÷ 15 min. = 32. Then, (32)(.75) = 24 trips

7. 24' ÷ 8' = 3; however, with a 2 ft. overlap, only 6' gets plowed. So, (24÷6)(4 min) = 16 min.

8. 23 cu.yds = 621 cu.ft. Then, (621)(100) = 62,100 lbs. Finally, 62,100 ÷ 2000 ≈ 30 tons

9. 8400 ÷ 150 = 56. Then, (56)(6 qts.) = 336 qts. = 8 gallons. Finally, 84 ÷ 42 = 2 drums

10. 5 tenths = (5/10)(12") = 6"

11. (54')(1/2')(10') = 270 cu.ft. = 10 cu.yds.

12. Volume = (10')(5')(4') = 200 cu.ft.

13. 3 hrs. 30 min. + 5 hrs. 30 min. + 4 hrs. 45 min. = 12 hrs. 105 min. = 13 hrs. 45 min.

14. 4296 sq.in. = 4296 ÷ 144 ≈ 29.8 sq.ft.

15. 11.8 tons = (11.8)(2000) = 23,600 lbs.

16. (72.5)(.75) = 54.375, closest to 54.5 gallons

17. (40 2/3)(3/4) = 30½ cu.yds.

18. (6')(5')(3') = 90 cu.ft.

19. $F = Wa/a = W$ lbs.

20. $F = (80)(2) \div 10 = 16$ lbs.

21. Mechanical advantage = 10/2 = 5

22. Specific gravity = $\frac{95-5}{50-5} = 2$

23. 1 meter = 100 cm. ≈ (100) ÷ (2.54) ≈ 39.4 in.

24. $1/4 \div 5/8 = \dfrac{1}{4} \cdot \dfrac{8}{5} = \dfrac{2}{5}$

25. 9:45 A.M. to 1:35 P.M. = 3 hrs. 50 min.

www.ingramcontent.com/pod-product-compliance
Lightning Source LLC
Chambersburg PA
CBHW082206300426
44117CB00016B/2692